The Contribution of Parents to School Effectiveness

D1386002

Edited by
Sheila Wolfendale and John Bastiani

David Fulton Publishers
London

David Fulton Publishers Ltd
Ormond House, 26–27 Boswell Street, London WC1N 3JD
www.fultonbooks.co.uk

First published in Great Britain by David Fulton Publishers 2000

Note: The rights of Sheila Wolfendale and John Bastiani to be identified as the editors of this work have been asserted by them in accordance with the Copyright, Designs and Patents Act 1988.

Copyright © David Fulton Publishers 2000

British Library Cataloguing in Publication Data
A catalogue record for this book is available from the British Library

ISBN 1–85346–633–6

Typeset by FSH Print & Production Ltd, London
Printed in Great Britain by the Cromwell Press Ltd, Trowbridge, Wilts.

Contents

Home and School - A working alliance

This series, edited by *John Bastiani* and *Sheila Wolfendale*, brings together wide-ranging contributions which

- are written from both professional and parental viewpoints
- offer an assessment of what has been achieved
- explore a number of problematic issues and experiences
- illustrate developments that are beginning to take shape.

It appeals to those with a special interest in and commitment to home-school work in all its actual and potential facets.

Series titles

Working with Parents as Partners in SEN
Eileen Gascoigne
1–85346–375–2

Home-School Work in Britain – review, reflection and development
By members of the National Home-School Development Group, edited by John Bastiani and Sheila Wolfendale
1–85346–395–7

Home-School Work in Multicultural Settings
Edited by John Bastiani
1–85346–428–7

Working with Parents of SEN Children after the Code of Practice
Edited by Sheila Wolfendale
1–85346–429–5

Linking Home and School: Partnership in Practice in Primary Education
Hugh and Jenny Waller
1–85346–682–1

Parenting Education and Support – New Opportunities
Edited by Sheila Wolfendale and Hetty Einzig
1–85346–579–8

Foreword

According to one of the editors of this book. 'Parents want the best for their children, in schooling, as in everything else.' The problem is that relationships between parents and schools are not uniformly productive. Where the relationship works well, both parties offer a great deal and the potential benefit for the child is huge. But both parents and teachers expect a lot and, if the reality fails to live up to the promise, either side can feel badly let down. This book investigates this critical relationship by drawing on accounts provided by academics who have worked with parents and practitioners responsible for parental involvement schemes.

The editors have assembled an interesting collection of writers who draw on North American as well as British research findings. They are not afraid to challenge assumptions or to recognise difficulties when these occur. The reality of the disadvantages that some families have to bear and the implications of this for schools, for instance, are clearly recognised.

The book adds to our knowledge of how children learn well. It also increases our understanding of schools and extends the definition of effectiveness. But, most important of all, it helps transform the theory of parental involvement into a practical approach to school management and the promotion of learning.

Peter Mortimore
London
January 2000

Biographical details of contributors

Contributors are listed in the order their chapter appears in the book.

Sheila Wolfendale has been a primary school teacher and remedial reading teacher, an educational psychologist in several LEAs and is currently Director of a Doctorate in Educational Psychology training programme at the University of East London. She has authored and edited many books, booklets, chapters, articles and handbooks on aspects of special needs, early years, and parental involvement. She was awarded a Professorship in 1988 and in 1995 gained a Ph.D. by published works. She has undertaken national and international consultancy in these areas.

John Bastiani is a freelance consultant on family-school matters whose work and numerous publications are both nationally and internationally recognised. He runs training and INSET courses all over the UK and beyond for professionals, parents and governors. He has been involved in several national development projects, evaluated many parental involvement initiatives and is currently working with RSA on their 'Redefining the Curriculum Project'. John is a part-time Senior Research Fellow at Nottingham Trent University and is the co-ordinator of the National Home-School Development Group.

John MacBeath is Director of the Quality in Education Centre at the University of Strathclyde. Over the past eight years he has been involved in research and consultancy for a wide range of bodies, including the Scottish Executive Education Department, The Prince's Trust, the Bertelsmann Foundation, the National Union of Teachers, OECD, UNESCO, UNICEF and the European Commission.

Much of Professor MacBeath's work in the last five years has been in the area of school self-evaluation, development planning and school improvement. He has worked closely with national governments and institutions in Denmark, Canada, Germany, Italy, Singapore, Uzbekistan, Hong Kong and Australia and with education authorities throughout the UK.

In June 1997 he was appointed as a member of the government's Task Force on Standards.

Beryl Bateson works for Birmingham LEA as the Family Involvement and Lifelong Learning Director in the Advisory and Support Service for schools, with a specific interest in Family Literacy and Family Numeracy. She has taught in secondary, primary, pre-school and adult education and training settings in England, mostly in Birmingham, and in Kenya. Most of her work over the past 15 years has focused on supporting and increasing parent participation in schools, with their own children's education and in learning for themselves.

Sue Barnes is currently School Improvement Adviser Family and Community Education with Leicester City LEA. She trained as a primary teacher with over 20 years in the classroom in a variety of school contexts, followed by 15 years as an Adult Basic Education worker and organiser. Her specialisms include family literacy, family numeracy and specific learning disabilities (dyslexia), and she is a national and regional trainer in basic skills education and family learning.

Bala Bawa is Learning Community Project Director for Newham LEA. Previously, as Newham's Parental Involvement Coordinator, she managed and coordinated the City Challenge Action for Achievement Project, before which she managed the Outreach team (home–school liaison). She was also a secondary school teacher with responsibilities such as Community Coordinator and Head of Year.

Angus Hardie is Coordinator of the Instep Project, based in Castlebrae Community High School. Professionally trained as a social worker, he has spent the last 16 years working in community development and urban regeneration initiatives. During the last six years, the focus of his interest has shifted towards schools and the development of more effective home–school relationships.

Margaret Alcorn is assistant head teacher at Castlebrae Community High School in Edinburgh where she has been a member of the management team since 1991. In February of 1999 she began a two year secondment to the City of Edinburgh Education Department as Principal Officer for the staff development and training of teaching staff.

Barrie Wade is Professor of English in Education at the University of Birmingham and, prior to that, he taught in both primary and secondary schools. He has a deep interest in the development of language in young children and in how learning takes place, and he still teaches regularly in schools. He has written books for teachers and more than 100 articles on language and story, special educational needs and language development and is also a widely read author for children, having published poetry, fiction and information books.

Maggie Moore is Director of the School of Arts and Social Sciences at Newman College, Birmingham. Prior to that she taught in primary schools and was head of an assessment unit, her interests being in psychological aspects of education and literacy. She too has contributed extensively to books for teachers in these areas and is a fiction writer for children. She has developed several wordless picture books for young learners.

Barrie and Maggie have been involved in promoting books for babies since the first Book Trust initiative in Birmingham in 1992. The conferences that they have participated in have attracted more Bookstart schemes and their evaluations and research have proved the value of an early start with books. In particular they have shown that time spent with infants and toddlers sharing books brings advantages when children start school.

Lisa Capper is Education Manager for CEDC (Community Education Development Centre), in a national charitable trust based in Coventry. She was responsible for setting up the Share project and other innovative family learning and lifelong learning projects. Her specialism is early years and prior to joining CEDC she worked on the Out of School Childcare initiative for Kids' Club Network. Lisa's career has been based in the voluntary sector and she has an MBA in Public Sector Management.

Ray Barker taught in London schools before moving into educational publishing and multimedia. He was Director of the National Literacy Association Docklands Learning Acceleration Project and then Director of Projects and Consultancy at the NLA, working on the first training materials for the National Literacy Strategy. He is now Managing Director of Advantage Learning Systems UK, and an author in the areas of literacy and technology.

Glen Franklin taught in inner-London and was Deputy Head of a Primary school in Greenwich before becoming Assistant Director of the National Literacy Association Docklands Learning Acceleration Project and then Assistant Director of Projects and Consultancy at the NLA, working on the first training materials for the National Literacy Strategy. She is now Literacy Consultant for the London Borough of Tower Hamlets.

PART 1

Chapter 1

Effective schools for the future: incorporating the parental and family dimension

Sheila Wolfendale

Introduction to the book

There are now, at the turn of the twenty-first century, many published books on school effectiveness/improvement and likewise, on parental involvement/home–school links. Whilst parental involvement is cited in the school effectiveness literature as one of the key factors, little has been written in the UK, specifically exploring this domain and the interface between factors around home–school that could promote school effectiveness.

There is a prime factor inextricably linked in these two domains and that is school/educational achievement. It is usually seen as the key outcome measure by which school effectiveness can be judged (e.g. by OFSTED inspection) but some of the parental involvement literature also cites pupil achievement as linked to indicators of home–school relations. 'Proving' these links has been notoriously difficult, since educational achievement or underachievement rests on a complex multifactoral matrix.

The present Government is investing in a number of educational and social strategies to raise and extend pupil achievement which involve parents. Examples include: the National Literacy Strategy and family literacy; the National Numeracy Strategy and family numeracy; SureStart, the early years intervention programme that involves parents; parenting programmes; education action zones, which are premised on partnerships between schools and local communities; baseline assessment and its component of reporting to parents; the introduction by all schools from September 1999 of home–school agreements. This commitment to involving parents in education is premised on ideological conviction as well as evidence to date.

This book is concerned with quantitative outcome measures, such as pupil performance, as well as qualitative 'value added' measures, such as expressed teacher, parent, pupil satisfaction on the nature of the working relationship between all of these 'stakeholders'. The two editors of the book, and the contributors, hope that it will be regarded as

- a celebration of proven success in home–school relations, contributing to school effectiveness;
- an exploration of factors surrounding educational achievement and the involvement of parents, carers and families;
- a contribution to the continuing debate on the pivotal relationship between schools and the families which form their constituencies.

Scope of the book

A number of the chapters describe contemporary innovations in home–school practice and seek to demonstrate that key outcome measures and defining criteria of the complex relationship between parental involvement and school effectiveness include enhanced pupil and educational achievement as well as less tangible indicators.

Chapters 2 and 3 affirm the difficulties of ascribing linear causal relationships between educational interventions and pupil achievement. The influences upon pupil learning (as manifested by measurable performance) impinge from all directions – from experiences and learning opportunities not only in school but from home, kinship and friendship networks and the wider community.

Parental involvement in education now has a pedigree of its own as a valid subject area and its history has been chronicled over a number of years (Wolfendale 1983, Wolfendale 1992, Dyson and Robson 1999). We can trace from seminal texts and project reports that the rationale of parental involvement has primarily focused upon raising educational achievement with ancillary aims including:

- boosting children's well-being by having their parents/carers and teachers working to shared goals on their behalf;
- enhancing teacher satisfaction that parents are supporting their endeavours;
- increasing parental knowledge of school processes and thus reassuring them that schools are doing their best by their children.

A myriad of small- and large-scale initiatives attest to these aims and demonstrate a range of outcomes that justify the original hypothesis expressed thus in the Plowden Report (1967) 'by involving the parents, the children may be helped' (Chapter 4). Such sentiments have pervaded education over the years, to the point where, nowadays, close working links with parents for many schools have now become routine and well established (Bastiani and Wolfendale 1996).

Yet, notwithstanding a raft of proven initiatives including government-backed ones, a number of schools have maintained a rather suspicious not to say distanced view of the benefits of closer working relationships and still regard too much parental presence within schools as an intrusion. First-hand contact and knowledge reinforces this assertion, that practice is still variable between schools and between local education authorities (LEAs).

But all schools and LEAs are now caught up with implementing their own development plans and applying effectiveness strategies. As stated, the school improvement and effectiveness literature includes home–school links as one of a list of criterion measures and it behoves all schools and LEAs to consider the evidence of 'what works' within parental involvement. The core mission of this book is to examine 'what works?', 'how do we know it works?'. This first chapter is discursive and considers the relationship between school effectiveness, home–school relationships, and pupil achievement, contextualised by a range of recent initiatives, reports, policy documents and legislation. The second chapter, by John Bastiani, closely examines 'varieties of evidence and degrees of proof' and proposes a working typology with examples to characterise a number of differing, possibly competing approaches.

John MacBeath in Chapter 3 provides a short review of school effectiveness and the relationship with homes and families, and critically examines components of 'the learning coalition'. His scrutiny culminates in bringing to readers' attention the American-derived concept of the 'full service' school which is the community locus for related agencies that provide services for children and their families. This is a model that is beginning to lap on to these shores – see towards the end of this chapter and the chapter by Angus Hardie and Margaret Alcorn.

The four chapters in Part 2 provide accounts of recent and current partnership practice within several local educational authorities. These accounts by Beryl Bateson, Sue Barnes, Bala Bawa, and Angus Hardie and Margaret Alcorn do not baulk at describing obstacles that have been overcome and residual problems in maintaining working relationships between schools and families that impact positively upon children's educational experience.

The focus of the three chapters that comprise Part 3 is upon literacy and learning, with empirically-based demonstrations of the impact on pupil achievement of parent and family involvement in the acquisition of crucial foundation skills, essential as prerequisites to later, indeed, lifelong learning. Barrie Wade and Maggie Moore describe the early years parent and carer-focussed Bookstart venture which has spawned many replications; Lisa Capper informs us of the Share 'parents as partners in learning' initiative which has been taken up by an impressive number of LEAs and primary schools; and Ray Barker and Glen Franklin tell us about the IT-based literacy programme targeted at a number of primary schools in the London Docklands area, within which the parental input was significant.

The editors and contributors hope that the book convincingly presents the 'value added' dimension, namely, the parental contribution to pupil achievement and school effectiveness, but does not shy away from considering the maintenance strategies needed to guarantee continuity.

This chapter now goes on to consider evidence-based practice, contextualises parental involvement, and explores the link between school effectiveness and parental involvement as a key 'alterable variable'. The notion of target-setting and measurement is then examined, with reference to current initiatives and this is followed by a proposition that organisational change/systems theory frameworks could be a useful applied approach. Finally there is speculation about ways in which the 'effective school' could evolve, encompassing best practice in home–school relations.

Towards evidence-based practice in home–school work: making the match

It is appropriate and consistent with moves within social and health care that educational innovations within the home–school realm should in the future be premised upon 'what works' or, in other words, evidence-based practice (EBP). Newman, in a National Children's Bureau/Barnardos *Highlight* information and discussion sheet (Newman 1999) describes a number of approaches to EBP in social work and intervention approaches in the early years which can include: randomised control groups, use of pre- and post-test measures, as well as systematic literature reviews, meta-analyses, canvassing users' and participants' views by means of surveys, focus groups.

Within education, some of these measures would be more ethical and principled than others. For example, a no-treatment control group *not* in receipt of a particular intervention might be viewed as inequitable, whereas full participation by parents and carers at all stages of a proposed piece of research could be construed as being consistent with equal opportunities partnership principles (see Wolfendale 1999 for a proposed Code of Ethics in this precise area).

As a body of evidence as to effective home–school practice accrues, researchers, practitioners, policy-makers, participating parents and carers need to learn and apply the lessons of antecedent endeavours. Over the past 30 years or so there have been countless home–school initiatives, the outcomes of which ought to be adding to the stockpile of what works, what does not, and leading us to more sophisticated research and practice methodologies.

The Joseph Rowntree report (Dyson and Robson 1999) provides an invaluable critical review of past innovations and myriad exploratory projects in the home–school-community area. Their sifting of the 'what works' evidence from several hundred sources enabled these conclusions (amongst others) to be reached:

- that many projects were short term, in time and money, and locally-determined, thus making longer-term effects and generalisations difficult to assess;
- the literature review yielded little about cost-effectiveness or cost-benefits of various approaches;
- the review affirmed evidence that involving parents in their children's learning (mainly in the spheres of literacy and numeracy in the primary years) is likely to enhance the attainments of children, to improve their attitudes to learning and to be welcomed by many parents;
- however, counterbalancing these promising findings, the authors found that there seem to be a number of problems that go largely unaddressed in project reports and the discursive literature, such as: dropout and attrition rates; non-significant gains in pupil attainment; longer-term follow-through; consideration of other influencing variables; ethical and political issues;
- the definition and operation of 'partnership' remains problematic; indeed as John MacBeath points out in his chapter, issues of the inherent imbalance of power between parents, carers and professionals from a range of agencies bedevil well-intentioned initiatives.

The message of this book for continued moves towards evidence-based practice echoes the call of Dyson and Robson for a range of rigorous studies into 'what works'.

Contextualising parental involvement: contemporary coalitions

Considerations of parental involvement vis-à-vis school effectiveness should first be contextualised within the 'bigger picture' in order to examine the interrelationship between within and outside school influences, and also to appraise to what extent the 'parents as partners in learning' ethos propagated from 'top down' government policies has pervaded educational and non-educational domains.

The vernacular shorthand for describing the current (Labour) government's commitment for harmonising a number of policy areas within and between departments at government and local levels is 'joined up' policies.

The area of parental involvement amply epitomises this pervasive policy. The mapping diagram (Figure 1.1) denotes broad areas (e.g. education, health, social services, voluntary/independent/community agencies) within which designated contemporary initiatives appear. Their presence within one of these broad domains indicates either (a) the primary funding sources, and/or (b) from where the initiatives emanate or *mainly* reside. However, the arrows show the inter-connections between the areas, reflecting perhaps joint, if not equal funding, shared vision and goals, personnel, procedures and outcomes. Also portrayed, centrally in the diagram, are a number of those initiatives which are national or come direct from government. Many of these are high-profile, with much money and high hopes invested in them. Amongst these are SureStart (an ambitious, multi-million pound-funded partnership venture between Education and Health involving early years support to parents), Parenting Education and Support, backed by Education and the Home Office (see Wolfendale and Einzig 1999), the National Literacy and Numeracy Strategies (picked up below) and Education Action Zones.

It is to be hoped that evaluation will automatically be built in to these projects, which will include quantitative and qualitative indicators of their impact and effectiveness.

Links between school effectiveness and parental involvement as an alterable variable

The presence of home–school as a key characteristic in the list of school effectiveness indicators comes as no surprise and, as John Macbeath says, now borders on the commonplace, so pervasive has the Plowden hypothesis, advanced earlier in this chapter, become. The discourse around what exactly comprises 'parental involvement', 'home–school links', 'partnership with parents' – terms which are often used interchangeably, even by the cognoscenti in the field – is extensive within the literature and is likely to continue, judging by the plethora of publications looked at by this author as part of the preparation for writing this chapter.

A single reducible fact distilled from such copious sources is that all researchers, practitioners, policymakers regard the parental/family dimension as a powerful 'alterable variable'. Bloom (1979) first identified how the influence of the home is one of five 'alterable variables' which can enhance educational achievement. An alterable

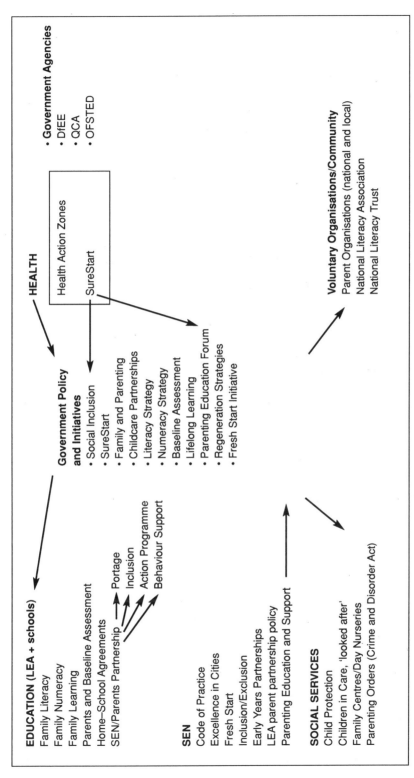

Figure 1.1 Working with families as partners in service delivery across agencies: the rich picture

variable is one that is not fixed or static, can be altered or manipulated. For example, home background as an influencing variable can be construed as a fixed determinant of educational achievement, i.e. as an unalterable variable, *or* it can be viewed as an influencing entity, possible to alter, and having benign as well as alleged pernicious effects on later achievement.

Peter Coleman uses alterable variables as a bedrock formulation too, as a starting point to describe his researches (Coleman 1998). He and other seminal North American writers, such as Joyce Epstein (1996) via models and taxonomies demonstrate the different facets of the parental and family contribution, rather as a prism refracts light at different angles. So, to recap from the literature, the parental contribution to education comes from and via such major dimensions as:

- the formulation and transmission to children from adult carers of beliefs, values, attitudes, including attitudes towards education, learning, career aspirations;
- the 'home curriculum', i.e. what opportunities, activities, conversations, etc., are provided from birth onwards;
- parental/familial engagement with school life, its routines, its learning opportunities and the reciprocal extension of these into the home via, for example, family literacy and numeracy programmes.

Each of these dimensions and their many constituent parts, as current reviews affirm (Dyson and Robson 1999, Hallgarten 1999–2000) have been operationalised into practice in thousands of school settings, and exemplify the power of this one *alterable variable*.

A table provided by Chrispeels (1996) entitled 'Comparison of Family Practices which support Children's Learning and Effective Schools Characteristics' provides a reciprocal view of 'Family Practices which support children's learning' on the left column and 'Effective Schools Characteristics which parallel family practices' in the right column. The lists in each column are mirror images of each other and encapsulate how the major dimensions listed above can be unpacked into a myriad of home–school reciprocal activities.

This conceptualisation goes to the very heart of the symbiotic relationship between school effectiveness and the key characteristic of parental involvement, since it is based on 'what works' culled from the literature.

Part of Bloom's intention in positing the influence of the home as an 'alterable variable' is to dispel the myth and received wisdom that 'difficult' hard to access families prevent teachers from forming successful working relationships with them. Parents and carers who are deemed to be 'different', because of ethnic diversity or low socio-economic status or being in a 'deviant' family configuration, or having special needs can often be held up by schools as being immutable stumbling blocks and impediments to successful school status.

Debate continues to rage as to whether schools can or should 'compensate' for familial or societal perceived shortcomings. Many intervention programmes are predicated upon a 'deficit' model and as such fail to acknowledge and incorporate the 'wealth' (e.g. of custom, tradition, language, kinship, friendship, mutual support) inherent in family networks.

The present Government is promoting a number of high-profile educational strategies such as Education Action Zones, Excellence in Cities (DfEE 1999), Regeneration Programmes (see Figure 1.1), to

(a) help combat the presumed effects of poverty; and
(b) enhance the involvement of ethnic minority families, often deemed to be at risk of marginalisation from the 'mainstream'.

Also, to boost educational achievement by under-functioning pupils, the literacy summer schools were started (Sainsbury *et al.* 1998). But Cook (1996) discusses the ethical and practical dilemmas that when 'special' programmes such as summer schools in the United States were introduced for this very purpose, their universal availability meant that the academic differential between advantaged and disadvantaged children perpetuated. Yet singling out certain groups for special attention may not be principled and the effects may be scientifically dubious.

A number of writers in the volume edited by Christenson and Conoley (1992) address this conundrum and propose various solutions, particularly addressed to working with ethnically diverse groups (their term) and socio-economically disadvantaged groups, amongst which are:

- an ecological/systems framework to facilitate targeted, but equitable home–school collaboration (Chapter 4 and see later in this chapter);
- application of anthropological and sociological perspectives which affirm family strengths and utilise these in home–school work, rather than emphasise deficits (Chapter 5);
- regarding family–school collaboration as 'a process, a philosophy that pervades everything you do in the school' (page 221, Chapter 10).

These strategies epitomise an 'inclusive' school which is robust enough to deal with diversity, including all family types as described above and what in Christenson and Conoley is referred to as the 'changing demographic tapestry' (page 81) as well as changing family compositions, and see Zill (1996). This has implications for the 'full service' school referred to by John MacBeath in Chapter 3 of this book and returned to towards the end of this chapter.

In dealing with presumed 'difference' and diversity, I want to emphasise this point: that a hallmark of an effective school is essentially one that can respond sensitively to its constituent families and can embrace them as partners in the educational enterprise. The concept of 'alterable variables' is an empowering and liberating one.

Weighing the evidence: evolving good practice

John Bastiani in Chapter 2 deals extensively with a range of different models of educational effectiveness and tackles concepts and sources of evidence. As he and John Macbeath in Chapter 3 confirm, post 1998 Education Reform Act (now, as with all educational legislation post 1945 up to 1996, subsumed into the 1996 Education Act) the entire education service has been targets and outcomes driven. For example, schools were urged by the DfEE and OFSTED to set targets to raise standards (DIEE/OFSTED 1996); OFSTED inspection has promoted the categorisation into successful and failing schools; the National Literacy and Numeracy Strategies have set targets for pupil performance in the short and medium term; LEAs, like schools have to produce Development Plans, with achievable goals, and are also now subject to OFSTED inspection.

The onus is on schools to face, Janus-like in two directions, simultaneously; one is the provision of tangible, quantified outcome measures, as required, the other is to satisfy a wider community, including pupils, parents, governors, other local stakeholders, that schools can deliver on all criteria.

If we apply the 11 school effectiveness criteria listed by Stoll and Mortimore (1995) with their accompanying division into 'School Improvement (facilitating conditions)' and 'School Effectiveness (the final picture)' we see that of necessity, many 'outcomes' can only and legitimately be judged in qualitative terms. (A reminder to readers – the list of 11 school effectiveness characteristics are: participatory leadership; shared vision and goals; teamwork; a learning environment; emphasis on teaching and learning; high expectations; positive reinforcement; monitoring and enquiry; pupil rights and responsibilities; learning for all; partnerships and support (this includes parental involvement).)

Fortunately some parental involvement measures, enshrined in recent educational legislation, such as Reporting to Parents as part of on-entry to school Baseline Assessment (mandatory since September 1998), the Home–School Agreement (mandatory since September 1999), the involvement of parents/carers in special educational needs assessment and intervention procedures (via the 1993, now 1996 Education Act, and accompanying 1994 Code of Practice) facilitate the production of qualitative indicators to complement quantitative targets, including pupil performance, as well as offsetting the most pernicious effects of a 'number crunching' approach.

A school's reputation for its approachability, the welcome it gives to parents, their inclusion in activities, is the 'whole' that is more than the sum of its parts. When these constituent parts are broken down and micro-analysed, it is difficult to pinpoint precisely the effectiveness of any one. Let me illustrate by a simple example: many schools have their school logo on artefacts, such as mugs, pens, T-shirts. Do these commonplace but useful objects signal 'parent friendly' messages; can we infer from their existence a school's philosophy and commitment to home–school relations; is their existence tokenistic, a superficial gesture, or is it reflective of a pervasive, wider and deeper active engagement with parents and families? What we can learn from such a constellation of possible 'hard' and 'soft' evidence is that if it is 'fit for purpose' – that is, illuminates an issue, answers the (research) questions, proves the efficacy of an approach (curriculum, intervention) – it is admissible, legitimate and part of a panoply of proof of what works.

Dyson and Robson (1999) in their review rightly point to flaws and inadequacies in many erstwhile parental involvement projects. However, what must be borne in mind in any appraisal of past endeavours is that so many were exploring new territory, with methods and instruments that were perhaps not fit for purpose, precisely because it was new territory, and what looks like naivety or ignorance now, with hindsight, was tentative trail-blazing at the time.

'No pain, no gain' – behind a bland, polished set of 11 school effectiveness characteristics (see Stoll and Mortimore 1995, and see above) lie all sort of painfully hard won lessons, educational 'experiments' that did not work, were not sustained, were abandoned.

Epstein, in a wide-ranging review (1996) regards these pioneers as paving the way towards more sophisticated successive waves of endeavour in the home–school sphere, to the point where, she avers, we can now prognosticate about directions in which future research, practice, social policy can cohere to best effect.

An organisational and systems approach to enhancing school effectiveness via home–school relations

A Preface and a Proposal: a construct that in recent years has gained in prominence and applicability is that of 'ecology', applied to schools and families. The theoretical formulation advanced by Bronfenbrenner (1979) is that each of us is part of social/domestic/educational/perhaps work place interlocking, overlapping 'ecosystems', and explanations of individual human functioning or dis-functioning are incomplete without analysis of how, why, where we are each juxtaposed within each of these systems or to put it most precisely, within our 'econiches'.

There is a conceptual link between this formulation and a view of schools as organisations and systems. In itself, the view that schools are organisations and discrete systems is well-established in socio-educational literature and is a prosaic observation to make. However, what offers potential is the marrying of the ecological with a systems approach and applying this combination to the home–school dimension.

Weiss and Edwards (1992) propose a model for their project which does incorporate these elements and they invoke the work of Tagiuri, who identified 'elements of organisational climate'. The project model delineated 'culture, milieu, social system and ecology', and against each of these four defined elements are listed practical applications.

British educationalists and home–school exponents would be familiar with many of these practical applications and activities delineated in the Weiss and Edwards' model. They include all the sorts of activities usually listed in home–school manuals and guides (for examples, see in the References section CEDC 1998 and the Newall Green Handbook, Manchester City Council 1998).

What is proposed in this chapter is an application of ecological/systems approaches to home–school work as one concerted and theoretically sound way of:

(a) ensuring high-quality home–school work, and
(b) in so doing, making a marked contribution to planned overall school effectiveness.

A rationale: it is axiomatic, as already stated, that schools are intact and dynamic organisations, comprising a number of interconnecting organic units and sub-systems (e.g. departments, subject areas, year groups, classes, each with identified personnel, pupils and staff, attached to them). In turn, the organisation connects when activated to 'outside' systems and sub-systems, such as families, the LEA, other agencies, shops, businesses, community organisations and institutions.

It is consistent with this image of a school to perceive that parents and families interact with some of the sub-systems some of the time, and that a systems analytic approach could facilitate understanding of: the interaction, its frequency, type, outcomes as well as of the endemic social forces, shifting power balances, tensions and contradictions between and amongst key players. Such analysis could be a precursor and catalyst to change. But a system is not a static entity; its organic motion is an inherent part of its functioning and a systems analytic approach acknowledges this dynamism and momentum and seeks, via its analytical tools, to explore interactions and conflicts.

How could systems analysis and organisational change be applied to home–school work and school effectiveness? Firstly, a reference to classic texts, such as Handy (1985) and Handy and Aitker (1986). Readers interested in pursuing techniques and procedures would, after consulting the salient literature, select methods that are fit for the purpose. Standard features of such approaches could include:

- auditing present practice, devising the audit from data from home–school work going on in the different school sub-systems
- using such analytical and problem-solving techniques as
  - quality circles (small groups which are collaborative, problem-solving)
  - SWOT (strengths, weaknesses, opportunities, threats) analyses
  - force-field analysis which promotes the close analysis of the socio-political context within the organisation, and facilitates identification of the power bases and power held/not held relationships between key players (teachers, non-teaching staff, pupils, parents, others), the 'actors' in the scenario
  - rich picture or 'ecomap', an imaginative diagrammatic representation of the perceived situation, showing sub-systems, key players, positives and negatives and power balances within their interaction with one another. A rich picture is flexible, adaptable, frees the compiler(s) from the rigidity of text on pages, facilitates creative and associative thinking. The use of pictures, cartoons, sketches, captions, quotations is an empowering tool in systems work.
  - From all the data and the analyses, it is possible to construct 'reality maps' and use these as a vehicle to (i) identify agreed goals and (ii) to effect change and development.

Readers are cross-referred to discussion in Brighouse and Woods (1999) of problem-solving approaches and 'appreciative enquiry' as relevant analytic tools (pages 146–7) and to MacBeath (1999) on school self-evaluation. Both these texts include the parental and home dimensions as part of their working models.

To convince readers that the systems/organisation change approach has some potential I will mention several home–school areas that have already been referred to in this chapter and which, as set out in educational legislation, require schools to respond. These are:

- home–school agreements;
- 'reporting to parents' within Baseline Assessment
- 'having due regard' to the SEN Code of Practice;
- developing family literacy and numeracy as part of schools' literacy policies (in turn, part of the National Literacy and Numeracy Strategies).

Although good practice in these areas can be found, it is at present far from being established routinely in all schools. A systems/organisational change approach could be applied to each and all these four key areas as well as home–school work in other areas.

Effective schools for the future: incorporating the parental and family dimension to best effect

This final section of the chapter attempts to weigh prospects for home–school relations in the 'effective school' of the near future.

A turn of the century school will, most likely, continue to be working towards imposed and prescribed educational targets, be subject to periodic inspections and be on the receiving end of inducements such as 'superteachers', 'learning mentors', and participation in Fresh Start, Education Action Zones or similar initiatives. Home–school activities will be expected to form a routine part of school provision. We can prognosticate some of these home–school activities, from the literature, from evidence, from educational legislation. We cannot, however, determine the extent or quality of this work.

At this point in time, as one century turns into another, we can also, cautiously, predict the directions of some school and family work. Two areas of probable significance will be singled out and discussed below.

1. Family learning and lifelong learning

That learning extends beyond school and is for life, that all of us have enduring learning needs and entitlements has become an universally accepted credo, encapsulated in a number of official documents. Although it is axiomatic that human beings do not cease to acquire information, knowledge and skills throughout an active life, proper recognition of this can ensure greater opportunities to fulfil these needs.

An intrinsic part of this lifelong and developmental conception is that home and families are as equally if not more so than school, a prime locus for learning. Indeed, contemporary home–school perspectives incorporate this fundamental ideology and the dynamic link between 'informal' and 'formal', schooled learning is expressed thus:

> the informal education that takes place in the family is not merely a pleasant prelude, but rather a powerful prerequisite for success informal education from the primary grades onward.
>
> (Bronfenbrenner 1974)

Titus Alexander (1997) perceives families as being 'the foundation of education' and family learning in his book refers to the vast amount of learning that takes place in and around families, from personal development, language acquisition and hobbies to the process of becoming a teenager, adult, parent, grandparent to taking on other family responsibilities. Alexander proposes a ten point national 'manifesto' of action to acknowledge this and to support families to fulfil their responsibilities. Schools are part of a nexus to support and develop all forms of learning; and see the Government's commitment to developing a national framework for study support and the vision that goes beyond the school gates (DIEE 1998).

The Royal Society of Arts (RSA) in its discussion document on redefining schooling (1998) says 'the flexible school should be a centre of community learning' (page 9) and its 1999 report on redefining the curriculum (RSA 1999) extends the vision whereby a radically revised school-based curriculum reflects societal needs in keeping with societal changes. The RSA competence-driven curriculum framework encompasses student learning needs that go beyond schooled learning into learning to cope and learning for life.

The part that effective schools will play goes beyond the older model of a community school to one wherein a school is part of a *partnership in learning.*

2. Schools as a locus for other service providers

Earlier in the chapter reference was made to the 'full service school' (and see Chapter 3). McDonnell (1997) forecasts the need for a different view of service delivery, in the light of recent developments such as Children's Service Plans and, latterly, 'joined up' thinking, to effect closer working links between agencies that provide services for children and their families. He proposes that integrating services through the school is about:

- a broad based community involvement
- addressing the needs of children through a constant organisational approach
- finding ways of making better use of existing fmancial and human resources
- building coordination and collaboration into everyone's professional training
- revised organisational systems that empower field staff to search out locally based responses and solutions
- flexible structures within an organised framework that promotes ownership of the decisions made
- community-based responses to the collective needs of children and families

(McDonnell 1997, page 134)

The slow, but it is predicted, sure growth of an idea much practised in New Zealand, namely, Family Group Conferences (Marsh and Crow 1999) is another example of a move away from traditional, totally professionally dominated service delivery (Wolfendale and Einzig 1999). The role of a learning mentor mentioned above and spelled out in *Excellence in Cities* (DfEE 1999) is another example of a bridge between schools and agencies.

These embryonic developments are compatible with the conception of an Education Action Zone, where school is a central location, but by definition, operates in partnership with families, other agencies, businesses, community organisations (DfEE 1997).

Recent educational and social innovations, a number of which have been mentioned in this chapter, and in this book, have had to include evaluation, quality assurance, accountability measures. Initiatives pump-primed with public money, have to be transparent and have to account for their successes and failures. Many criteria for 'effectiveness' have been advanced in this and other chapters. We can anticipate that schools and LEAs will have to keep pace with those related areas of family-friendly social policy, such as the creation of the Family and Parenting Institute and SureStart (Home Office 1998) which will impact onto the education service in due course. The effective school could become one in which 'parental involvement' as one of the key characteristics is seen to be pervasive and predominant.

References

Alexander, T. (1997) Family Learning, the foundation of effective education. *Arguments, No. 15.* London: DEMOS.

Bastiani, J. and Wolfendale, S. (eds) (1996) *Home–School work in Britain: review, reflection and development.* London: David Fulton Publishers.

Bloom, B. (1979) 'Alterable Variables, the new directions in educational research'. Paper presented at the Scottish Council for Research in Education, Edinburgh.

Booth, A. and Dunn, J. (eds) (1996) *Family–school links, how do they affect educational outcomes?* New Jersey: Laurence Erlbaum Publishers.

Brighouse, T and Woods, D (1999) *How to Improve Your School.* London, Routledge.

Bronfenbrenner, U. (1974) A report on longitudinal evaluations, Vol. 21s early intervention effective? Washington, DC, Department of Health, Education and Welfare, Office of Child Development (ERIC Document Reproduction Service No. ED093 501).

Bronfenbrenner, U. (1979) *The Ecology of Human Behaviour.* Cambridge, Mass.: Harvard University Press.

CEDC (1998) *Successful Schools: Parental involvement in secondary schools, a good practice guide.* CEDC, Woodway Park School, Wigston Road, Coventry CV2 2RH.

Chrispeels, J. (1996) 'Effective schools and home–school community partnership roles: a framework for parental involvement', *School Effrctiveness and School Improvement* **7** (4) 297–324.

Christenson, S. and Conoley, I. (eds) (1992) *Home–School Collaboration, enhancing children's academic and social competence.* National Association of School Psychologists (NASP), 8455 Colesville Road, Suite 1000, Silver Spring, Maryland, 20910, USA.

Coleman, P. (1998) *Parent, Student and Teacher Collaboration, The power of three,* London: Paul Chapman.

Cook, T. (1996) 'Inequality in educational achievement: families are the source, but are schools a prophylactic?' in Booth, A. and Dunn, I. (eds) *Family-school Links, How do they Affect Educational Outcomes?*, Chapter 7. New Jersey: Laurence Erlbaum Publishers.

DfEE (1997) *Education Action Zones.* London: DfEE.

DfEE (1998) *Extending Opportunity: A national framework for study support.* London: DfEE.

DfEE/OFSTED (1996) *Setting Targets to Raise Standards, A survey of good practice.* London: DfEE.

Dyson, A. and Robson, E. (1999) *School Inclusion: The Evidence. A review of the UK literature on school-family-community links.* York: Joseph Rowntree Foundation/National Youth Agency.

Epstein, J. (1996) 'Perspectives and previews on research and policy for school, family and community partnerships', in Booth, A. and Dunn, J. (eds) *Family–school Links, How do they Affect Educational Outcomes?*, Chapter 14. New Jersey, Laurence Erlbaum Publishers.

Gold, K. (1999) 'One stop shops for inclusion', *Times Educational Supplement,* 18 June, 23.

Hallgarten, J. (1999) *Creating stakeholder schools, family and school partnerships for a learning society.* Institute for Public Policy Research (IPPR) Project, 30–32 Southampton Street, London WC2E 7RA.

Handy, C. (1985) *Understanding Organisations.* Harmondsworth: Penguin.

Handy, C. and Aitker, R. (1986) *Understanding Schools as Organisations.* Harmondsworth: Penguin.

Home Office (1998) *Supporting Families, a consultation document*. London: Home Office.

MacBeath, J. (1999) *Schools Must Speak for Themselves: The case for self-evaluation*. London, Routledge.

Manchester City Council (1998) *Partnership with Parents in Practice, Learning from Newall Green Nursery and Infant School, Manchester, Welcome to our School*. Manchester Inspection and Advisory Service, The Acorn Centre, Royal Oak Road, Wythenshaw, Manchester M23 1EB.

Marsh, P. and Crow, G. (1999) *Family Group Conferences*, Highlight No. 169. London: National Children's Bureau.

McDonnell, V. (1997) 'The needs of children and families: integrating services', in Wolfendale. S. (ed.) *Working with Parents of SEN Children after the Code of Practice*. London: David Fulton Publishers.

Morgan, G. (1986) *Images of Organisation*. London: Sage.

Newman, T. (1999) *Evidence-based Childcare Practice, Highlight* No. 170. London, National Children's Bureau.

Plowden, B. (1967) *Children and their Primary Schools* (The Plowden Report). London: HMSO

Royal Society of Arts (1998) *Redefining Schooling*. Discussion Paper No. 6, RSA, 8 John Adam Street, London WC2N 6EZ.

Royal Society of Arts (1999) *Opening Minds, Education in the 21st Century*. London: RSA (address as above).

Sainsbury, M., *et al.* (1998) *The Evaluation of the 1998 Summer School Programme*. NFER, from DfEE Publications, PO Box 5050, Sudbury, Suffolk CO10 6ZQ.

Stoll, L. and Mortimore, P. (1995) *School Effectiveness and School Improvement*. Viewpoint No. 2, University of London, Institute of Education

Weiss, H. and Edwards, M. (1992) 'The Family–School Collaboration Project: systemic interventions for school improvement', in Christenson, S. and Conoley, J. (eds) *Home–school Collaboration, Enhancing Children's Academic and Social Competence*, Chapter 10. NASP, 8455 Colesville Road, Suite 1000, Silver Spring, Maryland, 20910, USA.

Wolfendale, S. (1983) *Parental Participation in Children's Development and Education*. London: Gordon and Breach Science Publishers.

Wolfendale, S. (1992) *Empowering Parents and Teachers – Working for Children*. London: Cassell.

Wolfendale, S. (1999) 'Parents as partners in research and evaluation: methodological and ethical issues and solutions'. *British Journal of Special Education* **26**, (3), 156–61.

Wolfendale, S. and Einzig, H. (eds) (1999) *Parenting Education and Support – new opportunities*. London: David Fulton Publishers.

Zill, N. (1996) 'Family change and student achievement: what have we learned, what it means for schools', in Booth, A. and Dunn, J. (eds) *Family–school Links, How do they affect educational outcomes?*, New Jersey: Laurence Erlbaum Publishers.

Chapter 2

'I know it works!...Actually proving it is the problem!': examining the contribution of parents to pupil progress and school effectiveness

John Bastiani

> Where parents and teachers work together and education is made a priority at home, children develop beyond their peers and beyond expectations. (OFSTED)

> I have become even more convinced that parents and teachers working together in partnership are able to bring out the best in children. (Teacher)

> When teachers, parents and children work together, everybody benefits – especially the kids! (Parent)

The enormous and continuing importance of home influences upon educational outcomes has been widely accepted for many years, although its real significance has not always been taken into account, either in government policy or in the everyday life of many schools.

The accounts in this book recognise and endorse the power of the key relationships between families and schools. However, they go beyond this to suggest a number of problematic and challenging areas that need to be acknowledged and tackled, in order that this valuable experience can be taken on board.

The previous chapter explored some of the ground that such an exploration would need to cover and suggested a number of different routes that might be taken. This chapter, by contrast, explores a number of issues of method and evidence – some of them for the first time – which characterise the field. Particular emphasis will be given to the development of an approach which is responsive to the needs of hard pressed staff in schools of all kinds, in a wide range of settings and circumstances.

In order to be considered as a key feature of a school, its work with parents[1] and carers will inevitably be evaluated in terms of the

---

1 The term 'parents' is used throughout this chapter as a form of shorthand for the diverse arrangements for looking after and bringing up children and young people in contemporary Britain.

prevailing criteria of the day. So the contribution of home–school work will be currently seen mainly in terms of its contribution to meeting school improvement targets and to individual pupil progress. There is, of course, more to this than meets the eye!

Contrary to popular belief amongst politicians and throughout the media, the assessment of both schools and pupils is an extremely messy and challenging business! This is true even of relatively straightforward areas, such as the assessment of the outcomes of direct teaching in classrooms. How much more true is it of the effects of an institution like the family,

- whose existence as a key player is recognised by many schools and teachers, but underplayed, or even ignored, by others;
- whose main influences take place before full-time schooling even begins;
- which exists independently of much of the everyday life and work of schools;
- whose responsibilities and influences are both wider and longer term than those of schools.

In trying to isolate, and pin down empirically, something of the wider influence of families and of their combined effects with schools, there are a number of major problems and difficulties.

Although family influences are both powerful and continuous, they are relatively hidden. Many schools know little and see less of the family lives and circumstances of the children they teach. While this is generally true, it is particularly heightened where family culture and lifestyle differs sharply from that of the class and staff rooms, where families lack confidence, do not speak English as a first language or have become disaffected through their own school experience (Bastiani 1998a).

Family life and circumstances are diverse, varied and can change profoundly. The opposite effects, for example, of active interest and support on the one hand, and instability and disruption on the other, can have a dramatic impact upon children's progress and well-being, in both the short and, often, the long term. This is illustrated graphically in the following example. As often happens, reading scores and records provide a fairly precise form of systematic evidence.

By the end of the school year, eight year old Eva had improved her reading by a staggering 32 points, from 102 to 134. Another eight year old pupil, Jack, went down the scale by 25 points, from 125 to 100. If Jack had been taught by Mr Green, Eva's skilful teacher, whose class improved by an average of more than five points during the year, would he have done better?

The astonishing truth is that he did have Mr Green. Jack and Eva, examples of two of the biggest rises and falls in a year, were classmates. Eva's mother supported her avidly, helping her produce a substantial book of her own writing. But Jack's home life disintegrated as his parents separated during the year. He was often absent and rarely concentrated in class, often seeming far away. *(Names have been changed.)*

(Wragg *et al.* 1998)

Educational strategies that derive from gathered knowledge about children's backgrounds and lifestyles, it goes without saying, need to be based upon sensitivity and tolerance, mutual trust and respect.

Interestingly, pictures of the educative life of real families, grounded in evidence, can turn out to be very different to those of teacher lore and classroom mythology! The present author has just completed the second of two annual Parent Surveys for an Early Intervention Strategy project in 11 schools in a Scottish urban authority, characterised by extensive social disadvantage and educational underachievement.

Contrary to what is often thought, said and written, the picture of the educative life in these, often hard pressed, families is encouragingly upbeat and positive. A majority of the parents and other main carers in the 11 schools provide regular encouragement and practical support for their children's school learning, are actively engaged as a family in a wide range of 'educational' activities, both in the home and throughout the wider community, and are involved in a range of opportunities that relate to their own learning and development.

Family influences are context bound in other ways too. As studies over the years have demonstrated, parents have an enormous range of viewpoints and experience; they have different information needs and differentiated opportunities for communicating with their children's schools; similar experiences will produce different responses and effects. Getting a fix on the contribution of parents and families to pupil progress and school effectiveness is further complicated by other considerations too.

The current scene

Government policy, supported by an ideology of school–family partnership (which has variable congruence with the real world!), stresses the common aspirations and goals of politicians, educational professionals and parents, together with the possibility of shared responsibility and joint action, currently exemplified in official guidance about home–school agreements, literacy strategy and homework.

There is, however, a growing body of evidence, derived from very different kinds of information and data (such as 'stakeholder' research and ethnographic studies of key events in family–school relations, like parents' evenings), which provides a very different view of the world. It stresses key *differences* between school and family perspectives and experience and portrays tensions that stem from contact as well as complementary roles and reciprocal responsibilities. School perspectives, too, increasingly focus upon the *short-term* outcomes of school effectiveness and pupil learning, through annually renewable targets, through Key Stage SATs and the apparatus of standardised tests and scores.

Families, by contrast, have signed up for the long haul! Parenting, famously described as the most challenging 'unpaid job for life' (Pugh *et al.* 1994), is committed both to long-term responsibility and the all round development of balanced personalities. Here, the 15/85 quote (children spend only 15 per cent of their lives between 5 to 16 years in schools) serves to place schooling as simply an *episode* in young people's educational lives, however significant, against the needs of personal growth and lifelong learning. There is an interesting and productive paradox here. Even as they are looking for success and effectiveness in rather narrow, quantifiable terms, major studies, such as the National Foundation for Educational Research (NFER) Family Literacy Programme Evaluation (Brooks *et al.* 1996), have uncovered substantial evidence of both wider benefits and longer-term developments (see Figure 2.1).

As well as illustrating tangible and lasting basic skills gains for all those involved, such findings, characteristic of intergenerational and family learning approaches, uncover the development of changed attitudes, relationships and behaviour in key areas.

Finally, the contribution of parents and families to the 'effective school', through their active support both for the school and for their children's learning, cannot get far without a brief recognition of the problems of definitions and values.

Faced with progressively narrowing targets and definitions of success, based on reductionist, input/output measures of factory-like productivity, many parents are beginning to see that schools are being obliged to go too far in this direction. When this happens families will see a *very* different role for themselves in constraining these unwelcome influences, in providing an antidote for excessive or over narrow demands and in stressing alternative sources of experience.

Compare the following:

Many have wanted us to portray our uniquely British love affair with the goals debate, rather than focus upon means, as school effectiveness research tries to ... (Precisely) because we did not waste time on philosophical discussion or on values debates, we made rapid progress.

(Reynolds 1998)

The importance of parental attitudes to a child's progress at school seems to be firmly established. Yet the concept of 'favourable parental attitude' is perhaps one of the most ambiguous and misleading in the contemporary discussion of educational achievement. The measurement of this attitude has been crude in the extreme; and precisely what has been measured is open to very serious doubt. It would be very dangerous indeed to equate parental interest and concern with kindly, beneficent and understanding encouragement. The usual measures of parental interest might equally signify ruthless, unreasoning, inexorable and even quite unrealistic demands.

(Musgrove, F. 1966, p. 76)

❑ The benefits to children (see Report).

❑ The benefits to parents (see Report).

❑ **Parents' ability to help their children, as follows**

  • There were *substantial increases in literacy-related home activities*, and these became *firmly embedded* in family practice.

  • Parents also reported *substantial increases in their ability to help their children* with language and literacy and in *their confidence* in doing so.

  • Parents seemed to feel that *a barrier between school practice and home activities had been crossed.*

  • Parents were beginning to *enjoy their own success as they saw their children's progress.*

❑ **Bonus effects,** which include

  – the lasting nature of the gains made

  – the marked improvement of communication between parents and their children

  – considerable subsequent improvement in the numbers of parents involved in their children's schools and in their ability to communicate with their children's teachers.

Such wider effects are clearly of longer-term, cumulative benefit to both children and their families.

(Basic Skills Agency 1996)

Figure 2.1 Selected extract from 'Family Literacy Programme: A summary of outcomes'

At the heart of this area lies the danger of seeing the 'effective', the 'good' school, solely in terms of high, or improving, SATs scores, league table positions, exam results, marks and grades. And the need for hugely neglected, wider debate about what schools are *for*.

Problems of conceptualisation and mindset are also to be seen in the often very public definition of 'unsuccessful' or 'failing' schools that have been part of the nefarious 'naming and shaming' strategy. Here 'unsuccessful' schools are assumed to be simply inferior versions of those in which pupils 'do well'. They have lower levels of the ingredients than they need to do well. Improvement is seen, therefore, to consist in increasing the dosage of conventional remedies.

However, a growing body of experience, particularly the more recent Fresh Start Initiative and Education Action Zones, both of which have scope and potential for changing the ground rules, suggest more promising territory: here, the possibility of introducing more relevant curricula, reorganising teaching and learning and assessing achievement more imaginatively, suggest the untapped potential of alternative approaches.

Much of the experience drawn upon in this book stems from schools providing statutory education in mainstream settings. This emphasis, however, contrasts with a range of concerns and experience, a familiarity with alternative agendas and complementary approaches, that are also a characteristic of the contributions in this volume. Here, a concern with the processes of mainstream schooling, is supplemented by an active engagement with wider agendas, which include accounts of active learning through different approaches and forms of provision, in a range of different settings. These include

- the learning of *very* young children;
- the progress of learners in bilingual/multicultural contexts;
- intergenerational learning;
- family and community learning;
- the blurring of roles and boundaries between education, care and development; classroom, home and out of school learning in homework and after school clubs, supplementary schools, supported study initiatives and enrichment courses.

Effective schools: effective families

There are obvious dangers in trying to identify the implications of 'effective schools' for the work of families simply by extrapolating aggregated lists of the common features of the highest achieving schools and transposing them into a family context.

This, to some extent, already happens. A school centric view sees family involvement and support solely in terms of the willingness and capacity of parents to support the work of teachers in the manner of schools and on schools' own terms (Chrispeels 1996). Within such a widespread and entrenched professional view, often implicit in a school's attitudes and practices, homes are increasingly regarded as outposts of school learning, progressively colonised through training parents in reading support strategies at school-based workshops, issuing homework guidelines, activity sheets and workbooks – some of the paraphernalia of informed parental support.

There are two main problems here. First, it progressively reduces the role of parental involvement to its subsidiary one of supporting the school's primary tasks, across a narrow achievement agenda. Second, it denies the distinctive, complementary nature of parental roles and responsibilities, disempowering parents by doing so. It also denies parents a genuine role in the process of shaping wider educational purposes.

Interestingly, light is thrown on just how 'effective families' operate on a day to day basis in a fascinating study by Clark (1983). In examining a sample of high-achieving black pupils from poor families, in a Chicago public housing project, he was looking at families who could be said to be successful, in social educational terms, very much against the odds. He found a number of common family practices made a significant contribution to their children's school success (see Figure 2.2).

Family Practices of High-Achieving Students

- Valuing schooling and developing a sense of pride and self-reliance;
- Establishing specific family routines such as homework time and bed time routines;
- Establishing family roles and responsibilities and assigning family chores;
- Supervising children's use of time, especially TV viewing;
- Encouraging reading, even if the parent was not fully literate;
- Talking with the child about schooling and other issues;
- Visiting the school and being an advocate for the child;
- Fostering hobbies and other extracurricular activities;
- Playing games together, visiting parks or museums or going on other family outings.

(Clark 1983)

Figure 2.2

It is notoriously difficult to predict or claim knowledge of the views of parents. Inevitably, however, broadly similar experience leads to a number of shared views. There is also a consistency about these views that applies to parents of children of all ages and in very different settings and circumstances. The following list is an attempt to identify the flavour and spirit of these:

Parents share many common expectations. They want

- The best for their children, in schooling, as in everything else. This means for most, a high quality, broad education, in a caring, effective institution.
- Regular, reliable and accessible information about what the school is doing and how this affects their children.
- Information, about their children's progress and achievements, about problems and, especially, help in identifying ways in which they can support their children's learning.
- Finally, most parents want to be taken seriously – to have a say and be listened to, to contribute to the life and work of the school and to their child's part in it.

(Bastiani 1995, p. 9)

Varieties of evidence and degrees of proof

'To be honest, it is hard work. But it's also very satisfying as you can see the improvement in children's work!' (Year 1 Teacher)

'I know it works. I just *know* it works! Actually proving it is the problem.' (Head teacher)

'Teachers can identify pupil progress beyond their expectations and in comparison with other pupils. What they cannot do is provide figures to support this.' (LEA Coordinator)

Newcomers to the systematic study of home–school relations (in Britain and, increasingly, through comparative studies) are often rather taken aback by the sheer *volume*, as well as the range, of published literature and research that is now available.

In this section a brief attempt is made to look at some of the approaches that are characteristic of the pupil achievement and school effectiveness agendas, briefly suggesting some of their strengths and shortcomings, but mainly with a view to identifying the elements of a practice-orientated approach. Like many typologies it is designed to stimulate comparison and contrast, doing so by exaggerating differences and making distinctions which, in the real world, are more blurred and indistinct.

1. The Standards and Effectiveness Model
(also see Figure 2.4 on page 30)

This is named after the major division at the DfEE, created by the current government after the last election. Its title brings together (but, interestingly, keeps separate):

- the major role of OFSTED and its uses of data derived from the formal inspection of schools;
- school effectiveness researches, and applied developments, such as the Hammersmith and Fulham LEA coordinated 'Schools Make a Difference' Project, which draw upon university based researches.

Through its close links with OFSTED and the Basic Skills Agency, it has a major influence upon both the Government's overall educational strategy and its work in specific areas, such as literacy and numeracy. This model is used by adherents without regard for discussion of ends and purposes, which are regarded as non-problematic. Ends are replaced by targets, rooted in aggregated data that has been standardised in large populations. Case study approaches are almost unheard of. 'School improvement', therefore, lies not so much in newer or clearer goals, or alternative approaches, but in target-setting, and measurable outcomes. It is a kind of 'evaluation' in reverse. Anything that produces improved results is to be recommended, adopted and implemented, without too much soul searching or further analysis

2. The Planned Development Model
(also see Figure 2.5 on page 31)

The 'planned development' model is based upon the view that change and development are reasonable and orderly processes! As such, it appeals particularly to administrators and senior managers throughout the educational service and in schools. School development plans often typify this. It gives emphasis to the consideration and clear statement of agreed principles and realistic goals. It also gives emphasis to the role of planning within a framework of planning, implementation and evaluation. In the event, most of the energy in new initiatives and developments often seems to go into getting something up and running. There is usually very little time, resources or energy left for maintenance, sustainability and further development.

Planned development approaches can be embodied in very different, apparently contradictory styles. Some additionally funded programmes, for example, work through a 'top down' approach, which is policy or project led. Others, like John MacBeath's work in the field of school self-evaluation, are 'bottom up', grounded in the systematic collection and comparison of data from the different 'stakeholders'. In both cases, a key feature is the development of quality indicators and criteria of effectiveness, against which progress and development can be assessed.

3. The 'What Works?' Model
(also see Figure 2.6 on page 32)

As its title suggests, the 'What Works?' model has wide appeal to practitioners, across systems and cultures (see OECD 1997), because of its explicit pragmatism.

It can accommodate a considerable range of different goals, approaches and outcomes, can suggest or be responsive to policy initiatives and can, for example, provide the basis for the exploration of a common, shared concern, in a wide range of schools and circumstances (see Bastiani 1995 and Cambridgeshire County Council 1999 Partners in Learning).

A 'What Works'/'Good Practice' model acknowledges that educational change can be a messy and unpredictable business, which has a strong human factor and in which different perceptions of the same experience can be influential. This model tends to see successful achievements as valuable and important in themselves and so their contributions to the wider picture are not always recognised. Any shortcomings are likely to be explained in terms of design faults or human and institutional failings that prevent proper implementation taking place.

Such a typology, however undeveloped, helps to draw attention to some of the differences of perspective and approach, that characterise different kinds of interest in the relationships between parental involvement and school effectiveness. For hard pressed teachers, however, they are more likely to suggest a number of elements that will need to co-exist, to be brought into a productive relationship in ways that can help them in their work.

Seen this way, an effective self-evaluation strategy would need to incorporate:

- The collection of a range of salient information and evidence. (There are many possibilities here, as Figure 2.3 shows.)
- A review of what has been achieved, against the background of stated aims and intentions.
- The need to identify, and take into account, the different views and experiences of teachers, parents and pupils.
- An approach which is formative and developmental, which gives emphasis to what can be learned from an examination of one's practice, that can contribute to improvement and progress.

To be effective, hard pressed schools and teachers will need to be able to operationalise this through a practical strategy which is a mixture of planned activity and positive opportunism. This will correspond, in part, to the mix of organised and informal contact that forms the basis of many home–school arrangements. It would need to be a continuous task (rather than something that is done as a one-off, or left to the end of the year), offering both minimal disruption and maximum usefulness. It would be rooted in a combination of available data and, above all, be an integral part of the professional mindset and everyday practice.

Collecting data: a checklist

Training materials: session notes.
Teacher logs, diaries and journals.
Evaluation materials and reports.
Photographic and video records.
The recorded views of parents (individual and collective): 'Juicy quotes'.
Completed Sharebook 'Comments': mini questionnaires.
Parent diaries: (additional material for accreditation purposes).
Pupil comments: examples of work.
OFSTED inspection reports.
On entry (baseline) records and ratings, individual profiles and cohort summaries).
– special tests (e.g. NFER, LEA frameworks and 'home made' measures), 'Before' and 'After' tests.
– teacher observations and records.
Special needs register (IEPs).
KS1 SAT scores.

(Bastiani 1998b)

Figure 2.3

Targets, performance indicators and success criteria

Differences of emphasis and approach in this area can be seen in a comparison of the following examples

Example of model 1: OFSTED criteria

This provides a summary of the views of a cross-section of teachers of the most relevant OFSTED criteria. These are themselves distillations of 'effective schools' research, progressively focused OFSTED inspection data, laced with political imperative and a dash of professional prejudice! Interestingly, in a teacher review of the *least important* factors that shape a 'good school', the most often mentioned are religious assemblies, healthy eating, pupils who do better than expected, complying with the National Curriculum and staff development. Figure 2.4 details an extract of OFTSTED's 23 criteria and key features (drawn from inspection data)

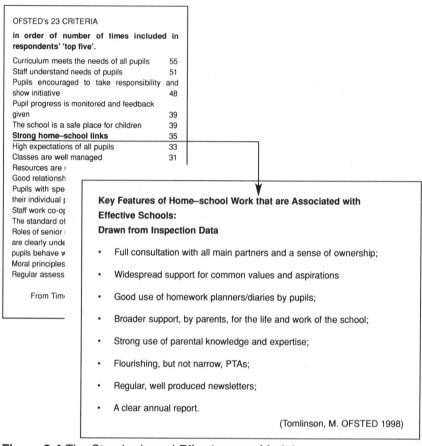

OFSTED's 23 CRITERIA

in order of number of times included in respondents' 'top five'.

Curriculum meets the needs of all pupils	55
Staff understand needs of pupils	51
Pupils encouraged to take responsibility and show initiative	48
Pupil progress is monitored and feedback given	39
The school is a safe place for children	39
Strong home–school links	**35**
High expectations of all pupils	33
Classes are well managed	31

Resources are
Good relationsh
Pupils with spe
their individual p
Staff work co-op
The standard of
Roles of senior
are clearly unde
pupils behave w
Moral principles
Regular assess

From Tim

Key Features of Home–school Work that are Associated with Effective Schools:

Drawn from Inspection Data

* Full consultation with all main partners and a sense of ownership;

* Widespread support for common values and aspirations

* Good use of homework planners/diaries by pupils;

* Broader support, by parents, for the life and work of the school;

* Strong use of parental knowledge and expertise;

* Flourishing, but not narrow, PTAs;

* Regular, well produced newsletters;

* A clear annual report.

(Tomlinson, M. OFSTED 1998)

Figure 2.4 The Standards and Effectiveness Model

Here, the dangers of extrapolation from raw inspection data are clearly illustrated. To many an eye, these characteristics are redolent of (secondary) schools in monocultural, suburban neighbourhoods. This, in turn, raises the issue of social background and 'effective schools'. High achieving schools (measured through reading and SAT scores, or five GCSEs Grades A–C) have very small numbers of children on free meals or from families living on benefit. Conversely, the larger the percentage of children on free school meals the more likely the school is to be underachieving and to be grossly over-represented amongst schools on special measures.

Example of Model 2: The work of the Quality Assurance Unit (former Strathclyde Regional Council)

Here, a coherent and systematic set of 'quality pointers' derived from a massive combined inspection and consultation process across the Strathclyde region, are brought together to provide a framework for school audit, self-evaluation and development planning. The exercise is underpinned by a broad policy commitment to a view of education in which relationships between schools, families and communities are seen to play a major role. Figure 2.5 shows an extract of the model.

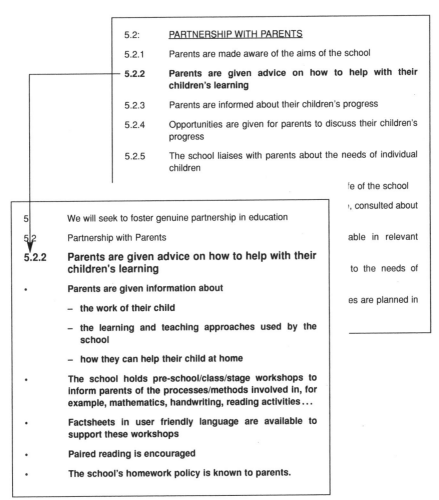

Strathclyde Regional Council (1992)

Figure 2.5 The planned development model

(a) What makes a 'good school?: a summary of parent views

- 'knowing where the school was going
- being reassured that their child was given the fullest opportunities to learn
- finding out how they could help their child at home
- being reassured that their child was fitting in and making 'friends
- being alerted quickly to problems either in learning or behaviour
- keeping open a channel of communication on a regular basis.'

(b) Key Features of home–school links: The combined views of parents, staff and pupils

- Parents play an active part in their children's learning
- Parents are confident that problems will be dealt with and feedback given
- These school provides for the social, cultural and linguistic backgrounds of pupils
- Parent–teacher meetings are useful and productive
- Pupil progress is monitored and shared with parents on a regular basis.

(MacBeath 1999)

Also see John MacBeath's chapter in this book

Figure 2.6

Example of Model 3. A 'Stakeholder Approach'

The weakness of any taxonomy of educational objectives, performance indicators or success criteria is that it is nearly always too inclusive and too orderly. But they do give hard pressed practitioners something to sink their teeth into, a starting point in the messy business of bringing goals and achievements closer together.

Disentangling the relationship between the contributions of parents and school effectiveness is an important, but challenging, task for schools which requires that different kinds of information and evidence are brought to bear on one another, that the views and experience of key partners in the learning process (including of course, pupils themselves) are taken into account and that the building upon sound judgements is part of a continuing and cumulative process. Above all, it is the *combination* of different kinds of views and evidence, with the opportunities that gives for cross-checking, that is so important. A basic list here would have to give priority to combining:

- formal grades and scores (derived from established classroom practice);
- the records, assessments and views of teachers;
- the views of parents;
- children's work and comments.

Of course, the appropriate 'mix' for this would need to be responsive to the age of pupils and the context of their lives. Very young pupils and those with acute learning difficulties and developmental problems in special schools present particular kinds of challenge; confident teenagers and disaffected school learners present others!

Additional opportunities to get glimpses of the educational lives of families are also provided by home–school diaries and by a growing number of courses for parents, located in primary schools, which focus upon the role of parents as co-educators. Here, the movement towards accrediting parental learning and experience, illustrated in several accounts throughout this book (see Lisa Capper's account in Chapter 9), provides opportunities and encouragement for the systematic collection of information, which can be enormously revealing.

In trying to bring home–school research and the development of effective practice closer together, there is still some way to go! The wider issues aired in the opening chapter, and the experience illustrated vividly in accounts throughout this book, endorse growing professional confidence that rigorous work in this area can, and should, be done. As a result there is a very underdeveloped but growing body of practical knowledge and understanding. We know, for example, that evidence of a parental contribution to pupil progress is more convincing when:

- There is a lot of it, it is consistent and suggests a clear pattern. This is particularly the case at the moment in the field of reading development.
- It is offered spontaneously, rather than being solicited. Quite simply, when parents tell us about things that have worked well for them, or not as the case may be, *without being asked*, that has special significance.
- It is also specific and detailed, rather than bland or general. This applies, too, when parental information can be linked to concrete contexts and activities. It might be a particular homework task or a comparison between two children at the same age.
- It has been systematically observed and recorded in lesson notes, teacher records, records of meetings or professional diaries. Or, the result of teacher research undertaken as part of a course of advanced studies in a local HE institution.

- The main partners (teachers, parents and pupils) are saying the same things, albeit in their own ways. At other times, of course, it will be *differences* between the accounts that will be significant.
- Different kinds of information and evidence are telling the same story – about individuals, groups and schools.

Most kinds of research emphasise systematic, formalised bodies of knowledge and experience and a corresponding interest in showing the patterns they contain. But there are other kinds of important evidence that are rather harder to pin down. They illustrate particular things – in context – for those 'in the know'! Their value has more to do with their *significance*, rather than their weight as evidence.

So, whilst evidence of general staff attitudes is valuable, when a particular member of staff takes a pro-parent stance, or volunteers to run a curriculum workshop for parents, in a subject department where this has never happened before, or the staff decides to invite parents to a training day, things can really be said to be beginning to hum a bit!

Some key issues

There are, within the scope of this book, a number of salient issues and concerns that need to be raised here. There is now, for example, abundant evidence that when schools can develop a practical working relationship with the families of the children they teach, there are tangible and lasting benefits in terms of pupil progress and school development. This is particularly true when schools are able to identify, and capitalise upon, the encouragement and active support of parents, carers and families. This is something of great significance and wide application. It is, in different ways, a matter of concern for *all* schools and *all* families. The everyday reality of life in many schools and families, however, often falls short of this.

In many schools staff can, and do, count on this support and often take it for granted; in others, in less promising circumstances, staff work hard to achieve limited success, involving parents more fully and obviously, although many families for a variety of reasons remain relatively untouched by their children's school lives. And there are still schools where parents are still consigned to the margins of educational life and to a minor, supporting role.

There are, here, big issues of access and equality of opportunity. Given what we know, schools clearly have a professional responsibility to try to reach as many parents and families as possible, by widening the range and appeal of their efforts. Schools have a clear responsibility to do everything they reasonably can to do the best for *all* their pupils. There are schools of all kinds and in every kind of circumstances who *are* managing to do this. But it is not easy and obviously cannot be done in five minutes! Above all, it requires genuine priority, fresh thinking and imaginative effort.

Clear, consistent and cumulative evidence about the contribution of parents to children's school behaviour, attitudes and academic achievement also carries clear messages that apply to all schools and all teachers. This applies not only to the coordination of collective efforts at the level of whole-school policy and approach, but also to the quality of contact and relationship between individual members of staff and the families of the children they teach.

A coherent and effective strategy in this area requires a number of strands. Firstly, if this work is to become a key, core task for all schools, it needs to become an integral part of the ways in which schools normally go about their main business. To do this, a school's work with parents and families needs to be, for example, a major, recurring item on the agendas of staff meetings, a feature of its planning and an area for INSET and professional development.

Secondly, there does need to be a clear policy, drawn up by, and including contributions from, all key partners, which contains a clear vision of what everyone is trying to do, together with negotiated policies and clear frameworks for practical action.

Thirdly, such an approach should embody an unequivocal commitment to the improvement of current efforts through the monitoring and review of existing practice and planned development in agreed areas. Here, some of the practical strategies outlined in this chapter come into their own.

Finally, an important ingredient in the evolution of effective home–school work, as it impacts upon pupil progress and school effectiveness, is that we move from a simple satisfaction from widening provision and increasing levels of participation, to issues of quality and effectiveness. We all need to develop clear frameworks and criteria that enable us to move beyond 'What' and 'How many...' to 'What kind of...' 'How well...' and 'How effective is...?'

A task as important as this requires at least the same degree of consideration and effort as the other key tasks and areas that contribute to a school's effectiveness and to its capacity to improve.

References

Bastiani, J. (1995) *Taking A Few Risks: Learning from each other – teachers, parents and pupils.* London: RSA.

Bastiani, J. (1998a) 'Guidelines to review and develop good practice in schools,' in *Family Upheaval and Change – A pack for schools.* London: National Stepfamily Association.

Bastiani, J. (1998b) *How Do we Know It's Working?* Share training materials. Coventry: CEDC.

Bastiani, J. (1998 and 1999) *Parent Surveys 1 and 2.* Evaluation of the South Lanarkshire Early Intervention Strategy – Home–School Strand. (Unpublished)

Bastiani, J. (1999) *Share: An evaluation of the first two years.* Coventry: CEDC.

Brooks, G. *et al.* (1996) *Family Literacy Works: The NFER Evaluation of the Basic Skills Agency's Demonstration Programmes.* London: Basic Skills Agency.

Cambridgeshire County Council. (1999) *Partners in Learning: Parents, children, teachers and schools.* Cambridge: Cambridgeshire CC.

Chrispeels, J. (1996) 'Effective schools and home–school-community partnership roles: a framework for parent involvement', in *School Effectiveness and School Improvement* **7**, 297–323.

Clark, R. (1983) *Family Life and School Achievement: Why poor black children succeed or fail.* Chicago: University of Chicago Press.

MacBeath, J. (1999) *Schools Must Speak For Themselves. The case for self evaluation,* 57. London: Routledge.

Musgrove, F. (1966) *The Family, Education and Society,* 76. London: Routledge & Kegan Paul.

OECD (1997) *Parents as Partners in Schooling.* Paris: OECD.

Pugh, G., De'Ath, E. and Smith, C. (1994) *Confident Parents, Confident Children.* London: National Children's Bureau.

Reynolds, D. (1999) 'The school effectiveness mission has only just begun', *Times Educational Supplement.* 20 February, 29.

Strathclyde Regional Council (1992) Mission Statement. 'Fostering Genuine Partnership in Education'. Tables 5 and 5.2. Glasgow: Strathclyde Regional Council.

Tomlinson, M. (1998) Notes taken from an address to the CEDC Successful Schools Conference, March 1998, London.

Wragg, E. C., *et al.* (1998) Extract from *Improving Literacy in the Primary School.* Research findings of the Leverhulme Primary Improvement Project. *Times Educational Supplement,* 9 October.

Chapter 3

New coalitions for promoting school effectiveness

John MacBeath

Entering a new millennium, we are still seeking a model of school education which will meet the needs of all children. This chapter argues that such a model of effectiveness is ultimately elusive because of the immense responsibility carried by parents and community. Illustrations of home and school work are drawn from research and development into homework and home learning. On the basis of both school effectiveness and ethnographic evidence, the chapter concludes that alternative conceptions of effectiveness will need to be found in new coalitions, new means for educational partnership.

For almost the entire history of the human race, responsibility for education lay with the family. School, a comparatively recent invention, has never fully succeeded in its role as an educational agency for all our children. Even in the first year of the Third millennium we find ourselves – policy-makers, academics, practitioners – still engaged in the search for a model of schooling that will meet the needs of all children.

This has been described as the hunt for unicorn, the search for 'the effective school', a singular term which seems to imply that, with enough investment in research, we will eventually track down this mythical entity and find its universal application. If a singular exemplar school could not be found, we might at least be able to identify the constituent parts, the key features of effective schools from which a model might be constructed. So, for three decades researchers have, with increasing precision and sophistication, sifted the evidence to identify the essential characteristics of those schools which performed best for their heterogeneous student bodies.

The search began in earnest in 1966 with James Coleman and a large team of American academics who set out to examine how well schools served the whole spectrum of needs of children growing up in a highly unequal society. Their conclusion was pessimistic. Published in a voluminous work entitled *Equality of Educational*

Opportunity, (Coleman *et al.* 1966) the team's conclusion was that school effects were marginal compared with the substantive effects of family and community. In other words, what children brought to school with them was a strong predictor of what they left with. Seven years later a team from Harvard University, led by Christopher Jencks, reached very similar conclusions. The report, *Inequality: A Reassessment of the Effects Family and Schooling in America*, concluded:

> Our research suggests that the characteristics of a school's output largely depend on a single input, namely the characteristics of the entering children. Everything else – its budget, its policies, the characteristics of the teachers – is either secondary or completely irrelevant.   (Jencks *et al.* 1972, page 256)

This was devastating confirmation for what many teachers and parents intuitively felt. It was particularly acute because the late 1960s and early 1970s had witnessed a massive critique of school failure and a plethora of best-selling titles such as *The School Crisis, School is Dead, Compulsory Miseducation, Death at an Early Age*, and Ivan Illich's highly influential *Deschooling Society* (1971) which argued for the abolition of school as we know it to be replaced by 'convivial networks', home- and community-based education.

With school occupying such a central place in the social and economic landscape it was inevitable that the thesis would be met by an antithesis and, perhaps by the advent of a new millennium, a synthesis. The antithesis may be represented by a sequence of studies bearing titles such as *Schools Can Make a Difference* (Brookover *et al.* 1979) and *School Matters* (Mortimore *et al.* 1988). The focus of these studies have been less directly with the Coleman/Jencks question 'Can schools reduce social inequality?', or with the Illich question 'Can schools educate?', but with the question 'Are some schools more effective than others?' Is there evidence that sending your child to school A rather than to school B will make a significant difference to educational success?

For policy-makers, pursuing this question is of far greater interest than the sweeping generalisations of researchers or the theorising of romantic rhetoricians. In the Thatcher-Reagan years, school effects studies were a priceless gift to government because, if evidence could be found for the differential effectiveness of schools, it could be put to the service of parental choice. It could, through the operation of the market, reinforce 'good' schools and put pressure on less good schools to compete or close shop.

School effectiveness studies, now so numerous world wide as to defy comprehensive meta-analysis, have generated many lists of key characteristics, most agreeing on a substantive set of core items. A selective analysis of the most rigorous studies, commissioned by OFSTED from the Institute of Education in London (Sammons, *et al.* 1994) identified the following eleven:

1. shared vision and goals
2. a learning environment
3. positive reinforcement
4. concentration on teaching and learning
5. monitoring progress
6. a learning organisation
7. professional leadership
8. home–school partnership
9. purposeful teaching
10. high expectations
11. pupil rights and responsibilities.

For researchers this is useful confirmation and a platform for further work. For teachers and school managers it may appear as little more than common sense. For parents it may raise more questions than it answers but, with relevant opportunity and support, may lead to further inquiry and fruitful home–school dialogue. For policy-makers and policy-implementers, such as the commissioning agency OFSTED, it provides a ready-made checklist which can be put to the service of school inspection.

However useful and important this research has been, it is fragile if not handled with care and even dangerous in the wrong hands. The wrong hands are those which make the research the handmaid of preconceived ideology and distort its findings in a way that undermines the efforts of teachers and impoverishes the role of parents. For example, the following passage from the Chief Inspector of Schools has a beguiling face value.

> I do not accept the argument that a child who has a free school lunch is a child who will necessarily find it difficult to read... If they are fortunate enough to have it [a good teacher], then, as test and inspection evidence shows, there is no reason why they cannot do as well as children from more privileged backgrounds.
>
> (Woodhead 1998, page 11)

The tabloid simplicity of this claim conceals a deeply disingenuous view – that good teachers can make all the difference. It implies that reading is 'taught' in school, defying all research (and common sense) evidence which demonstrates that the groundwork for reading is laid progressively in the five years or so before school, including the months before conception. The straw man who would claim a link between a free school meal and the ability to read, can be summarily demolished, but there is not a shred of research anyway to disprove the powerful association between poverty and school attainment – of which free school meals is a rough proxy guide.

Digging more deeply still into the evidence, we discover that poverty of itself is not the cause of learning disabilities. Poverty does not preclude the possibility of a culturally rich home environment. While the multifaceted nature of poverty makes it much more difficult, it does not preclude parents engaging in conversation with their children, reading to them, listening to them, helping them explore their world and helping them to structure it in a way that will smooth the transition into the formal structures of classroom learning. This is what the Israeli researcher Reuven Feuerstein (Feuerstein *et al.* 1980) described as 'mediation', the critical factor in effective learning. The struggle to survive as a lone parent with a large family, inadequate housing, ill health and few support networks is likely to inhibit opportunities severely for the kind of mediation which Feuerstein describes. If teachers, for their part, have to struggle to teach reading and then carry the blame for failure, we are doing a serious disservice not only to teachers but to children and parents too.

James Coleman, whose team of researchers set in train the effectiveness debate in 1966, continued until his death to explore the connections between home and school education. One of his most revealing findings (Coleman, *et al.* 1966) is that a key factor in school success is the opportunity that exists *outside* school to be part of a heterogeneous community where adults, young people and children engage in a common enterprise. He cites churches as one example of a structured community which provides a social arena for multi-age interaction, in which people feel a responsibility for other people's children, and in which there are opportunities for children to exercise multiple roles.

Peter Hannon (1993) offers a provocative contrast between the contexts of home and school, revisiting and reinforcing the Coleman/Feuerstein themes of the vertical age group and multiple roles. As Hannon's comparison suggests, the transition between these two quite different environments is not one that all children will slide effortlessly through.

School	*Home*
• shaped by curriculum	• shaped by interest
• bounded by sanctions	• spontaneous
• timetabled	• flexible
• contrived problems	• natural problems
• restricted language	• everyday language

School	*Home*
• limited conversations	• extended conversations
• special resources – limited access	• 'natural' resources – unlimited access
• recognition of achievement in approved areas	• recognition of achievement in many areas
• horizontal age group	• vertical age group
• distant relationship with adults	• close relationship with adults
• pupil role	• multiple roles
• accounts for little variation in academic achievement	• accounts for much variation in academic achievement

One of the interesting features of the above table is potential reversibility of some of the items – language, conversation, relationships, recognition of achievement, and vertical groups. Some families may be deficient in these and some schools can offer opportunities for a more familial environment. But what is clear from the work of Coleman and others, the home–school relationship is a dynamic one which cannot be reduced to a simplistic maxim of 'parental involvement' or 'home–school partnership'.

Home learning and home work

In the mid 1980s we were commissioned by the Scottish Education Department, as it was then, to undertake research into home–school relations. For a year and a half we conducted in-depth interviews with parents in their own homes, sometimes with their children present. Although scheduled for one hour hardly one of the hundred interviews lasted that length. Typically they lasted two to three hours and occasionally three to four hours as parents became more and more engrossed in the issues which they had, in most cases, never explored at depth with someone whose primary purpose was simply to listen and try to understand. Not to be lectured, interrogated, moralised with or harangued was for some parents a quite new experience and explained their initial caution and setting of time limits on the interview.

The more homes we visited and the longer we spent in each the more we came to appreciate the uniqueness of each new context. When two parents were present (or parent plus boyfriend/girlfriend), the interplay between the partners added a further layer of complexity to the dynamic of the home. Trying to tune into the secret harmonies and discords of family life gave us a vivid insight into the child's world, and provoked the question 'How do children and young people make sense of the two realities of home and school?' Interviews with children on their own, individually and in small groups, helped us to deepen our understanding of how they managed the changing expectations, pressures, contradictions and tensions of the worlds they moved in and out of. For many it clearly required a high level of resilience and self-esteem.

The roots of motivation, expectation and self-belief were on display. What young people took with them into their schools were belief systems which cast them as main or subsidiary players, powerful or powerless, helpless or masterful. What they brought back from school to home was homework, study, advice on course and career choice, school reports mapping their past, present and future, telling them what they were good at and not good at, and often what they *were*.

Many pupils in that study enjoyed the benefits of private tutors, expert or supportive parents. Some young people never did homework or study and lived in homes bereft of reading material of any kind. Some had a structured family life, while others enjoyed a completely laissez-faire environment. Some had strict and demanding standards of achievement and behaviour set for them, in some cases with firm consistency, in others with erratic unpredictability. It gave a new meaning to 'value-added' because it was clear that the tuition and support that children and young people got, whether from parents, older siblings, or from private tutors, was the real source of the value being added. It also challenged the very concept because there was not an additive but a dynamic interrelationship between home and school learning.

It was evident from that study that the best efforts of school effectiveness researchers to document the key variables that added value would always be partial and misleading without this illuminative insight into how 'value' was added or subtracted in the home. Hannon's work (1993) again illustrates that, in some instances and in some respects, parents can be more effective than school teachers. With reference to reading he concluded that:

- preschool teachers seriously underestimated the value of parental support for children's reading;
- the quality of children's experiences reading to their parents were in some respects superior to what happened in school;
- home readings were longer and had fewer interruptions than reading sessions in the classroom;
- parents' relationship with children allowed them to relate what they were reading to children's experience;
- teachers used praise more but it was often a mechanism of control and a reflection of their more distant relationship with the child.

Indeed it raised the question of whether for some young people schools actually subtracted value from the educational richness of what happened in the home.

Homework and learning out of school

When we were commissioned a few years later to carry out a study into homework we had a ready-made context in which to set our further enquiries and, replicating the research methodology we had employed previously, we found homework to be a much more problematic concept than policy-makers would have us believe. Homework can, of course, be quite simply defined as the pieces of work which teachers prescribe for children to do in their own time, but, as we had already learned, support and context for home learning is the crucially significant factor.

Once again, visiting homes and talking to parents we were able this time to focus more closely on how children learned, what they did when left to their own devices and what role parents or others played in the process. Some parents demanded homework be done, and done at a time and in a place that they saw as most appropriate. In other cases they made cursory enquiries and accepted lame explanations or left it to their children's initiative, perhaps accompanied by codicil such as 'It's her life. She has get on with it.' A few parents didn't appear to care too much whether homework was undertaken at all and made no demands on their children.

These home visits afforded us the opportunity to observe children at work, in front of the TV, with their Walkman on, on the phone to their friends, helping younger sisters or older brothers, teaching their teddy bear what they had learned that day. Some older children taught their younger preschool siblings so that they came to school not only able to read but confident self-assured learners. What we learned from this was just how different individuals are not just in terms of how they learn but the physical and social contexts where that learning takes place. Yet the advice which parents received from school betrayed a lack of understanding of that world of the home curriculum in all it complexity.

Among the findings of the study were these:

- the purpose of homework had not been clearly thought through or communicated effectively by teachers;
- pupils had not learned or been taught skills for self-directed learning;
- there was little support to hand at the time when pupils needed it (when they hit a snag or problem);
- the role and potential of parents as educators was undervalued and little understood;
- there was no regular systematic feedback to pupils, or to parents, on the quality of their work;
- there was a lack of diagnostic and formative assessment to guide parents and pupils on strategies for improvement.

The evidence from our research into homework pointed to something much deeper than dutiful completion of assigned tasks. It revealed an underlying failure on the part of schools to think through relationship of in-school to out-of-school learning. The challenge, for us as researchers, went a lot deeper too. It meant moving from the research and reporting to work with teachers and parents. This meant finding forums and strategies which would help people to explore the commonsensical everyday language which was often a mental block to genuine involvement. Deeply constraining concepts like 'intelligence' and 'ability' needed to be undone and alternative forms of language found. Homework needed, therefore, to demonstrate a quality of learning which demanded thinking, which was active, multidimensional, exploratory and social. This meant exploiting opportunities for pupils to share an idea, pose a question, teach something to a brother or sister, friend, grandparent or parent. Two examples from schools which decided to tackle the homework issue in new ways illustrate a shift in thinking and a shift in relationships.

A Scottish example

In Aberdour Primary School in Fife, a parent evening was planned to address the issue of continuity of learning between home and school. Aberdour parents strongly supported the practice of homework but had spent little, if any, time in thinking through the criteria by which the quality of homework might be judged. A meeting was arranged for parents with the inducement of wine, cheese and other goodies at the end of the evening and feedback on the homework questionnaires which they had filled out a few weeks before.

As parents entered they were met with large sheets of poster paper on the walls of the assembly hall containing various descriptors of homework drawn from pupil and parent questionnaires –'exciting', 'really fun', 'mundane', 'horrible', 'tiring', 'nice when Mum helped'. Other posters had lists of tasks from parents and pupils with examples of homework, such as 'We made puppets at home and then made up plays about them', 'We had to go home and with our parents to make a list of spices in the cupboard', 'Finding out how many inches there were in the Forth River'. Parents were asked whether they thought these descriptive adjectives and examples came from a parent or child.

This provoked a stimulating exploration of assumptions, prejudices, inert ideas and set the stage for a closer look at, not homework, but learning. Parents circulated in groups around a series of tables, trying out a range of different kinds of activities, problem-solving, analysing, categorising, talking, listening. The tasks had been selected carefully to be enjoyable and challenging. Before leaving the activity and moving on to the next table the group was asked to record their rating for the interest and value of the activity and to write a few key words on the skills they had needed to use to undertake the task set.

This was followed by a discussion which attempted to tease out from the activities some of the principles of learning, considering how these could be applied to home work. Parents were then referred back to their own descriptions of homework and the things they had enjoyed and benefited from as children. This gave the basis for arriving at a shared understanding of purposes and principles and offered a useful base on which to construct a programme of monitoring and evaluation. The term homework was ditched in favour of 'School Home Activity Research Exercises', or 'Share'.

This contrasted dramatically with what happened in another primary school in the project. In this school parents were invited in for a similar purpose but the evening started with a brainstorming session in which the head teacher asked for, and recorded on a flip chart, all the things that parents expected of the school in terms of homework. It provided her with a list of all the things she did not want – two pages of reading, five spelling words, ten sums. Perhaps it should have been foreseen that parents, without a challenging and stimulating catalyst, would reach back into, and endorse, their own experiences of homework.

Both examples illustrate the importance of dialogue, as well as the quality of dialogue which can extend and sharpen awareness for teachers as well as for parents. This is the basis of the learning coalition. This is the challenge to school effectiveness. It has to break the boundaries of the black box and redefine the nature of the relationship between learning in, and out of, school. It has to bring into new focus the quality of learning and teaching in the classroom.

A Canadian example

There are close parallels in the British Columbia schools investigated by the Canadian Peter Coleman (1998). Through questionnaires and interviews with parents, students and teachers he distinguished different kinds of parental support and influence. There were variations in three key dimensions – expectation, mediation and intervention. His case studies illustrate the strong presence or, in some cases, complete absence of 'aspiration-building' on the part of parents. The strength of these expectations are correlated with student expectations and commitment but that is not the whole story. The second factor is mediation.

Mediation describes what parents did to support their children's progress, not only in terms of the home curriculum but also in relation to the school, keeping in touch with the teacher, with the curriculum and expectations of homework. There was again a quite marked range of difference in parents' attitudes and skills in mediation, from those who took a consistent and persistent interest in what the school was doing, to those who seemed unconcerned about the lack of information from the school and were resigned to their child's loss of interest and application. Knowing what to do, how to do it and why it is important seemed to be the absent factors in these parents' repertoire, however much they wished well for their children.

The third category – intervention – describes the most proactive of parental responses. Intervention could take a variety of forms – close and careful monitoring of school and teachers, pre-empting potential difficulties, for example, by asking for a change of class, ensuring effective channels of communication, establishing expectations of homework. Intervention could also be reactive, taking the school to task over ineffective teaching or unprofessional behaviour on the part of the teacher.

Coleman suggests a number of typologies:

- The persistent parent, actively engaged in the school, using a built-up stock of knowledge and contact to mediate and intervene in her child's interests.
- The anonymous parent, seeing him or herself as a nonentity and unimportant in teachers' eyes and content to let the school get on with it.
- Parent as home teacher, acting in a compensatory capacity, taking on the role of teacher, developing techniques for teaching the child at home.
- Parent as reluctant mediator, recognising that the child needs help and that there are opportunities for intervention with the school but reluctant to take action, perhaps because it may be seen as detrimental to the child.
- Parent as ineffective advocate, trying to mediate and intervene but without success, feeling rebuffed by the school.
- Parent as skilful and experienced mediator/intervener, establishing excellent relationships and communication flow between home and school and between parent and child.

Taken together, expectations, mediation and intervention are clearly a dynamic combination. They are, however, complex in the way they are expressed because it is in the nature and quality of the interaction between parent and teacher, home and school, that the chemistry works.

It is in 'the power of three', as Coleman subtitles his book (1998), that student achievement, progress and commitment has, ultimately, to be understood.

We could depict a triangle of influence with parent, teacher and pupil at each apex with a plus sign on each of the three sides to denote a strong positive educational relationship – parent–child, parent–teacher, teacher–pupil. Substitute a minus sign on any one of these three sides and the power is diminished.

It is not simply in the physical relationship of the three key partners that the school effect or family effect is manifested. Coleman illustrates ways in which the 'family effect' is the ever present but invisible shaping influence in the classroom. Levels of student achievement and commitment, he concludes, tell you more about the home than the school and, he argues, 'Asking students to rate their schools is to ask them indirectly to give a report about the influence of their homes' (page 22).

The Coleman study is important and useful and, however different the British Columbia context, the themes are clearly paralleled in Scottish, English, Welsh and Northern Ireland schools. We might take issue with some of the apparent overstatement, for example on the student rating of their schools and teachers which, we have found, can be very positive by children whose home life is unhappy and unsupportive and find the school environment a positive and challenging milieu. We must also be aware of the 'anti self-fulfilling prophecy', the determination by some children to do well simply to defy the negative predictions of teachers or parents. We have seen a sometimes inexplicable resilience in children who find inner resources to rise above school or home influence. And, of course, there is the school and teacher effect where, in spite of all else, an inspirational teacher or stimulating school can have a dramatic impact on some individual children.

One of the issues with strong parallels in the United Kingdom is the power and status issue. Underlying the 'power' of three is the inherent tension, the invisible power play, that is constantly at work beneath the surface of the three sets of relationships. 'Partnership' is a term much used in Ministerial rhetoric, a feel-good word concealing the asymmetry and disequilibrium in the home–school relationship. What all but the most self-confident of parents experienced was the power of teachers, either in face-to-face meetings on a parent evening or as experienced at second-hand through their children's experience.

In the *Home from School* study (MacBeath *et al.* 1986) the power issue was a recurring theme, expressing itself most tangibly when it came to issue of territory. Our first awareness of this came through our interviews, conducted wherever parents chose – in school, home or a 'neutral' venue. Where it was held significantly influenced the nature of the interview and the relationships between parent(s) and interviewers. When we came on to the parents' grounds the dynamic of the relationship changed. If at times we felt like unwelcome guests it reflected a mirror image of what parents can feel like in the school or classroom.

In the course of the research we also accompanied teachers on home visits. There was a marked shift in the balance of power. Teachers were anxious about home visits and trod carefully when on unfamiliar ground. One home teacher, reflecting on the change in the power relationship, commented:

> The fact that you are meeting the family in their territory rather than your own "power base" relieves you of much of your false power in their eyes. If they are going to respond to what you say it is going to be because of what you say and not because you are a big powerful school.   (MacBeath *et al*. 1986, page 251)

School effectiveness revisited

The publication of *School Matters* (Mortimore *et al*. 1988) was a significant milestone in school effects research. It showed that some schools can and do make a bigger difference to the lives of children than others. The choice of school or luck of the draw can be the difference between success and failure. Follow-up research by members of that original team (Sammons, Hillman and Mortimore 1994) have added a more textured understanding to how school matters and to whom it matters most. They identified 'differential' effectiveness, showing that within most schools there can be both excellence and aridity, effective and ineffective departments, good, mediocre and bad teachers, productive, unproductive and conflicted relationships with parents.

But effectiveness is not only what common sense would have told us, the product of the differential quality of teachers. It works in more subtle ways than that. Within the same school, the same classes and with the same teachers, some groups of pupils do better than others. Some show spurts of achievement, some reach a plateau and stay there. Others regress. Some individual pupils thrive with a teacher while their companions fail to engage. Girls tend to do better than boys and perform significantly better in some subjects and marginally better in others (Thomas and Mortimore 1994).

Because the follow up to *School Matters* was a longitudinal study it was able to show ebbs and flows over time. For example, as pupils moved up through the system, the influence of socio-economic background became more pronounced. Ethnic differences played out in complex and unpredictable patterns. For example, children from a Caribbean background lagged further and further behind in reading attainment in the junior school years but in secondary the trend was reversed. In secondary schools, children of Chinese, Indian, Pakistani and Bangladeshi origin make better progress than their white peers.

Contrary to findings from other studies, research by the Association of Metropolitan Authorities (Thomas, Pan and Goldstein 1994) found that schools which obtained higher than average results for the most able (in other words, 'more effective' schools) were *in*effective for the least able. For the purposes of research categories such as 'ability', 'class', 'ethnicity' and 'gender' are treated as independent variables but in the real-life context of schools and classrooms it is the interrelationship of these that counts. When we study individual cases, for example, the experience of a low attaining English middle-class girl with parents of Indian background, we discover a dynamic and volatile set of factors at work. The nature of the peer group, the experience of racial or sexual harassment, tensions within the community, parental and teacher expectations, all work together and can change on a day to day basis. The exit of one or two key pupils and the influx of others can have a dramatic effect on classroom composition.

The 'compositional effect' as it known is a researcher's term to refer to the dynamic critical mass, the point at which individual achievement falls or rises depending on who your peers are and how many of them are high or low achievers. As Douglas Willms (1985) showed in the Scottish context, when high-achieving pupils leave, some of the school's positive energy source is drained off. Further, when high-achieving pupils leave to go to a 'better' school, they may also take with them the invisible parent that Coleman describes. They take with them the mediating and interventionist parents whose influence on the school may be an important irritant source or a catalyst for improvement.

A review of recent research (Gillborn and Gipps 1996) provides a rich and detailed picture of the intersect between individual experience and school life and illustrates how far we still have to go in our understanding of the internal culture of the school and how it connects, in multiple, interwoven strands, to the world of home, family and community.

The effectiveness research, taken in conjunction with ethnographic studies of family and community provide a frame of reference for teachers to probe more deeply into learning in their classrooms. It can also lead them into a more profound understanding of learning that takes place out of school.

These insights can be put to the service of management. They can help to reassess whole-school policies, with regard to attendance and truancy, home–school communication, parent meetings, homework, study support, special needs. They can be made accessible to parents to give them a broader, deeper understanding of the power of three and their own potential as parents to make school better.

In England the introduction of Education Zones has been aimed at defining a new relationship between school and community. In Scotland 'new community schools' are a radical attempt to provide a more family-directed service, a coalition of 'services' aiming at a joined-up approach to care, welfare and education. This is a Tartan reincarnation of 'full service schools' developed in America as a response to the compartmentalisation of social, health, employment and educational services, which often seemed more adept at serving the needs of the professions than those of their clients.

The full-service school brings together (ideally under one roof) the range of agencies whose job it is to serve families and communities, making it easier for professionals to meet, to share their knowledge and to respond flexibly and swiftly to issues as they arise. The concept of 'full service' recognises that needs do not come in neatly separated compartments – intellectual needs, health needs, psychological needs, social needs and that the three A's – attendance, attitudes and achievement – have their roots in family and community.

Whether we move in the direction of bringing families more to the school or take schooling more into the community, the key to effective lifelong learning in the twenty-first century will be to find new coalitions, new conceptions of school effectiveness, new meanings for the words 'educational partnership'.

References

Brookover, W. *et al.* (1979) *School Social Systems and Student Achievement: Schools can make a difference.* New York: Praeger.

Coleman, J. S., *et al.* (1966) *Equality of Educational Opportunity.* Washington D.C.: Office of Education.

Coleman, P. (1998) *Parent, Teacher and Student Collaboration: The power of three.* London: Paul Chapman.

Feuerstein, R. *et al.* (1980) *Instrumental Enrichment: An intervention programme for cognitive modifiability.* Baltimore: University Park Press.

Gillborn, D. and Gipps, C. (1996) *Recent Research on the Achievements of Ethnic Minority Pupils.* London: London University Institute of Education.

Hannon, P. (1993) 'Conditions of learning at home and in school', in *Ruling the Margins.* London: University of North London Institute of Education.

Illich, I. (1971) *Deschooling Society.* New York: Random House.

Jencks, C. *et al.* (1972) *Inequality: A Reassessment of the Effects of Family and Schooling in America.* New York: Basic Books.

MacBeath, J. (1994) *The Homework File*. Glasgow: The Quality in Education Centre, SOED, HM Inspectors of Schools.

MacBeath, J. and Turner, M. (1991) *Learning out of School*. Glasgow: University of Strathclyde Jordanhill.

MacBeath, J. *et al.* (1986) *Home from School 3: keeping in touch with home*. Glasgow: University of Strathclyde Jordanhill.

Mortimore, P., Sammons, P., and Ecob, R. (1988) *School Matters: The junior years*. Salisbury: Open Books.

Rutter, M. *et al.* (1979) *Fifteen Thousand Hours: Secondary schools and their effects on children*. London: Open Books.

Sammons, P. (1993) 'Findings from school effectiveness research: some implications for improving the quality of schools'. Paper presented to seminar series *Improving Education: The issue is quality*, Birmingham University School of Education and Birmingham LEA.

Thomas, S., Pan, H. and Goldstein, H. (1994) *Report on the analysis of 1992 Examination Results: AMA Project on Putting Examination Results in Context*. London: Association of Metropolitan Authorities.

Williams, J. D. (1985) 'The Balance Thesis – contextual effects of ability on pupil's "O" grade examination results', *Oxford Review of Education*, **11** (1), 33–41.

Woodhead, C. (1998) 'What Makes a Good Teacher?' Parliamentary Brief, p. 31.

PART 2

Chapter 4

INSPIRE

Beryl Bateson

INSPIRE (Involving School Parents in Reading and Maths) is a Birmingham LEA initiative evolving from several years' experience in parent partnership projects and builds upon considerable experience of family literacy and family numeracy work. Its most striking feature is its scope. Where many other projects have worked with small numbers of parents in relatively few schools, this initiative stretches across the whole of this large city and its various communities and aims to engage with all of the families of all the 370 primary schools and nurseries that choose to be involved. Another outstanding feature is its success in involving large numbers of parents, particularly those that schools say do not traditionally get involved and parents who have not been seen before by the school. So far, 140 schools have begun this approach; at least 8,000 families have participated in the last two years; and it has succeeded in engaging with fathers, and families from ethnic minority communities.

One experienced head teacher recently observed that INSPIRE is turning the whole city round in terms of parental involvement. Many experienced teachers have commented that they have previously tried all kinds of projects to involve parents, but this has been the only one that has really worked. This chapter will outline how we have made this happen and the context of the work within the Local Authority plans and Government policy.

Background – where it started

In 1991–3 the LEA ran a 'Leading to Reading' Campaign to raise the awareness of parents and communities across Birmingham of the importance of their role in the literacy development of young children. It involved producing leaflets with photos of national celebrities, notably an Aston Villa football player and stars from the TV soaps, holding story-telling events in public places and running workshops for parents of children under five years. Specific messages about literacy development were identified. These included: giving children role models of readers; sharing rhymes and stories; books and environmental print; ensuring access to writing; and developing oral skills through sustained talking. These key messages were threaded through a wide range of activities and were promoted through a video for parents. The workshops were structured around reinforcing these same key messages.

In some primary schools the workshop approach for parents and children was extended and ran throughout Key Stage 1 and Key Stage 2, involving class teachers more closely in the planning. These became pilots for INSPIRE and were very successful, generally involving 40–90 per cent of the families in each class.

In 1996, the Birmingham Core Skills Development Partnership was formed between City Council Departments (particularly, Education and Leisure and Community Services), Birmingham TEC (Training and Enterprise Council), Birmingham Voluntary Services Council and the national Basic Skills Agency. Its aim is to raise the levels of literacy and numeracy across the city for all age groups. One important strategic objective relates to engaging parents and families in this process. This initiative gave an increased momentum to a whole-city approach to INSPIRE, as an activity that was sustainable, could be implemented city-wide, and demonstrated the potential for impacting directly on pupil attainment levels.

Historical context

The culture of our schools throughout their history so far, has been to take children away from their homes to be educated by professionals and, in the best interests of the children, the door between home and school was usually firmly closed. This culture was deeply embedded and progress towards working with parents advocated in the Plowden Report in 1968 and later in the Bullock Report (1975) was extremely slow. Various vital research projects and initiatives of the 1980s, particularly PACT, Parents and Teachers and Children (Griffiths and Hamilton 1984), began to make their mark in examples of good practice scattered throughout the country and many of us relied heavily on the evidence that they offered. But we were still swimming against the tide. Tim Brighouse and John Tomlinson (1991, page 8) wrote 'it still remains the case that too many parents are told "to leave it all to us" in their first encounter with a school'.

Individual schools were testing out practice, but if sufficient impact was to be secured, there needed to be a major effort to motivate and support schools to come together behind a determined movement to get this ball rolling.

Culture change

There are all sorts of barriers that prevent parents and schools from working closely together. Understanding the strength of this embedded traditional culture and the essential need for change, was important in the motivational approach of INSPIRE. Appreciating that the context in Birmingham and nationally was beginning to change and recognising that the time was right, greatly helped in persuading schools, even self-confessed cynics, to give it a go.

Nationally the range of early initiatives had built up into a set of clear, new expectations. Sally Tomlinson (1991, page 3) observed that:

> There is now considerable interest in reversing the historical separation of home and school.

and

> Any government concerned to raise standards will concentrate on enhancing parental support, involvement and obligation to participate in their children's schooling.

Neil McClelland (1997, page 152) wrote:

> An urgent and concerted national campaign is needed to support the home and encourage more parental confidence and involvement. No parent should feel, as some undoubtedly do, that they are not, or cannot become, sufficiently skilled to make a contribution to their children's literacy development.

In Birmingham, a school improvement framework was adopted which emphasised the importance of seven processes, discussed by Tim Brighouse and John Tomlinson (1991). One of these processes is the involvement of parents and communities. Engaging with parents was clearly part of our common language for school improvement alongside leadership, management and teaching and learning. Involving parents is now recognised as an essential tool for improving the effectiveness of our schools; it is seen as something that can make a real difference.

Some national changes were supporting the developments being driven forward in Birmingham.

Engaging with parents became one of the aspects for government inspections of schools through OFSTED, and parents were consulted on their views of their children's school and the extent to which they felt involved. A national 1997 analysis of OFSTED data showed that progress in English is highest in schools with good parental involvement. Even in schools with high levels of free school meals – where fewer schools had good parental involvement – better progress was made in English in those schools with good parental involvement than in those schools without.

The National Literacy and the National Numeracy Projects that began in 1996/7 recognised this and included work on involving parents. The National Literacy Strategy (DfEE 1998) outlined four aspects of involving parents: informing, involving them at school, involving them at home and offering support through workshops and courses. The National Numeracy Strategy piloted leaflets for schools to give to parents, outlining targets for their children each year and suggesting supportive activities that could take place at home.

After being piloted by the Basic Skills Agency and researched through NFER (Brooks *et al.* 1996), Family Literacy Projects have been Government – funded through GEST and the Standards Fund since 1997. The allocation of funds directly to this area of work again validated the belief that families make a difference. In 1999, this was joined by opportunities for grants for Family Numeracy. Birmingham has been at the forefront of these activities as they developed and INSPIRE has been part of the city's wider interagency approach. The Moser Report (Moser 1999) to the Government on improving Basic Skills in this country recommends Family Literacy in all primary schools in disadvantaged areas by 2002.

Further indications of the importance of parent participation came in the launch of the Quality Mark for schools awarded by the national Basic Skills Agency. This includes an element of involving parents, for which schools have to provide evidence of their current practice. Birmingham has been enthusiastic in supporting schools to work towards this quality mark.

The School Standards and Framework Act 1998 required home–school agreements to be in place from September 1999. While these have a wider focus than literacy and numeracy, they bring an additional structure and emphasis to the work.

It was now clear that parents were officially on the agenda; involving the family, working with parents as partners has become an essential. Interest had been roused, motivation was high *and* we had a very successful model of good practice. We could start to turn this important juggernaut around!

INSPIRE – the model

Aims

The title INSPIRE reflects the underlying approach. The project aimed to change the prevailing attitudes and expectations of parental involvement in order to engage them in literacy and maths with their child and raise levels of achievement. At one extreme there was a belief that parents were the problem; that parents do not want to be involved; that parents are not available to be involved; that they have too many other commitments or too many other problems or priorities. Many acknowledged that parents often do not have the confidence to be involved in school or to help in their children's education; that they may have had bad experiences in education themselves; that they may not have had access to knowledge on how to be involved or that they needed their information to be updated; and that not all teachers or all schools make it easy for them to be involved. These barriers run alongside practical difficulties such as no available accommodation in school, little non-contact time for teachers, no child-care facilities for younger siblings and, with some families, no common language with which to communicate.

And so, we had to INSPIRE school staff that involving parents really could make a difference and it really is worth making this a priority; but more than this, that all the real and perceived barriers outlined above are not as great as imagined and not insurmountable. Once highlighted the barriers can be targeted and removed and we can move forward.

Teachers had in turn to INSPIRE parents and families about the value of what is done or can be done at home that supports the child's learning; and the simplicity of many valuable activities that can be initiated or encouraged by them, often more effectively in the home and community context than in school.

This approach is key to the project's effectiveness. The schools are not given prescribed lessons or materials to deliver; and the focus of the workshops is not seen as 'training' for parents. Although important, this was felt to have limited appeal to parents and leads to a different ethos and a different set of relationships between parents, teachers and children. INSPIRE is offered purely as an opportunity for parents/carers to work with their child alongside the teachers and be involved in activities that support their child. This is what we believe parents do really want. Staff are given time, personal encouragement and some vital general principles with which to create success. Through the experience, parents and teachers are both given the confidence that they can engage with each other with positive results.

The aims of INSPIRE are:

- to achieve more effective partnerships between school and home;
- to enhance and increase the opportunities for learning in and through the home;
- for schools to share with parents information about teaching and learning in school;
- to contribute to raising achievement in literacy and maths.

The model in action

The model is an extremely simple idea made effective by employing particular principles and approaches that have been identified as bringing success. Targeting one class at a time, each child invites a parent, grandparent, uncle or aunt, childminder or neighbour – a special adult – to come to support them in an activity in school (a workshop). The teacher prepares practical activities for the families to complete, with a particular literacy or maths objective in mind. The teacher sends supplementary publicity to each parent emphasising the fun, activity approach and the need for someone to come. Staff also speak individually to parents, whenever or wherever they can see them, to encourage them to come. Some schools telephone parents to encourage them to come and talk through ways of overcoming any difficulties that they might have in attending.

The best time of day for the workshop has been as the children arrive for the morning or afternoon session. The parents gather in the hall, spare classroom, community room or wherever the workshop is being held. They may have drinks, and informally meet the teacher or head teacher and a small selection of any other 'school friends' that they might know, such as governors, school helpers, religious leaders, local librarians, community workers, who will chat and make them feel welcome.

The teacher briefly explains the activities, either before or after being joined by the children; this will depend on age and concentration abilities. Previous preparation of the children can also make the experience more effective. They may have seen examples of the end-products – the masks, the puppets, the games – discussed their choice with the teacher or at home, practised the rhymes or the song, researched the topic with their parents, chosen a favourite book or identified reference books, selected spellings or tables to practice, or collected packaging or photographs from family and friends.

The families then choose, collect the resources from points around the room and complete the activities, while staff and helpers join different groups, tables or families, offering support, discussion and a spare hand where needed. Parents may chose one or several activities and then may take materials home to make others.

One teacher commented about INSPIRE, 'When you look at it on paper it does not look much. But, by gosh, when you try it it really works!'

Content of workshops

It still holds true that we remember most of what we do, but remember only a few gems of what we are told. Most of the workshop consists of practical activities: making games, books, puppets, masks; playing games, following trails, performing songs, rhymes, plays, shows. The sophistication and challenge of the activities depends very much on the experience of the school and parents and the stage of the parent–school partnership. Simplicity is very important, particularly at the beginning and especially with the more reticent families; although with appropriately planned support much can be achieved as confidence grows. Flexibility is also essential so that parents can build on knowledge and skills that they and their children are comfortable with. Each activity should allow for differentiation. It helps to give a choice from various examples, or to allow families to choose their own way of completing a task, rather than aim to produce 30 identical copies of one end-product where comparisons can be so obvious and confidence-destroying. It also should be fun!

Since the ultimate purpose is to raise levels of achievement, each workshop has clear, targeted literacy and numeracy objectives. These are multifarious, but always reflect or support what is being taught at that time in the classroom to those particular children. The message may be general, such as emphasising the use of environmental print, or having fun with numbers; or they may be quite specific like making a game to use for learning each week's key words, or making number lines or squares for numeracy homework, or working together to retrieve information from various sources. They therefore frequently correspond to targets of the present National Literacy and Numeracy Frameworks.

LEA Support

The approach applied is part of what the LEA offers in its overall school improvement drive, outlined in the Education Development Plan. This ensures that such developments are linked to wider LEA strategies and other strands of LEA provision.

To support and encourage schools in implementing INSPIRE, the LEA offers: an induction day for the head teacher and key members of each school phase, in-school support with planning and preparation for the first workshops, the costs of extra staff during the morning or afternoon of the workshop and a review session where groups of teachers evaluate their experiences.

The focus of the whole process for school staff is professional development. It is not solely training to deliver a particular package of activities, but practical support and encouragement to apply positive attitudes to working with families, to increase their skill and develop the confidence to apply their own knowledge to building to effective strategies which will thus facilitate a partnership with the parents of the children in their class.

Impact of INSPIRE

INSPIRE is evaluated against its four aims with both quantitative and qualitative evidence. This is collected from the training records, from group review meetings and workshop record sheets completed by all participating schools, from parents' and teachers' comments and from questionnaires sent to 80 schools that had run at least one session.

In aiming to achieve more effective partnerships between school and home, the goals were to involve the majority of parents in activity in the school and to improve the working relationships between teachers and parents.

Prior to adopting the INSPIRE methodology, many of the schools have been involved in some activity that attempted to reach parents, discuss children's learning and progress and give parents the skills to be able to extend their children's learning. These activities were usually having limited success in terms of reaching the majority of parents, in reaching the parents not normally seen by the school and maintaining a focus on improving the child's learning, rather than having adult training targets.

Reviews of the outcomes of INSPIRE show that over a two year period of the project, over 8,000 families have been involved; of these 25 per cent were from minority ethnic backgrounds and 15 per cent were men. By April 2000, a conservative estimate is 12,000 parents involved. This is an enormous difference to numbers that were usually attending such events. Schools reported an increase from an average 0–5 per cent of their parents/families involved to an average, at present, of 40–60 per cent (see Figure 4.1). Significant numbers of schools reported 95–100 per cent families involved through INSPIRE. Forty-four per cent of the schools surveyed were still embedding workshops as part of a whole–school approach and were therefore predicting further increases over the next six months. Fifty per cent have already established these workshops throughout the whole school.

An initial induction day has been attended by 330 teachers, including 74 head teachers and deputies, discussing issues, building confidence and experiencing the practice of involving parents. Major feedback showed that staff now feel more able and confident to work with parents.

A whole wealth of evidence has been collected that shows a positive attitude by parents and staff to the experience of the workshops and the difference they have made to home–school relations. The examples that follow are drawn from comments on teachers' workshop record sheets and from recordings of review meetings of groups of schools. These capture the flavour so effectively and are frequently spoken with excitement and great enthusiasm.

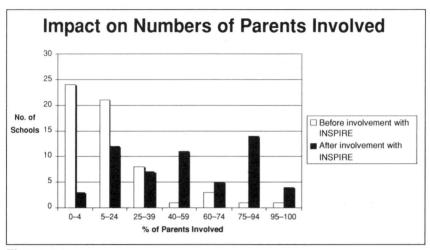

Figure 4.1

Staff/school

'It was a good way to get to know the parents and lovely to see so much interaction between parents and children.'

'I can't describe how wonderful it was. It was lovely. Really brilliant.'

'We have forged links with the majority of parents.'

'We haven't had anything work like this before.'

'We were astounded at the talking going on between parent and child.'

'Parents were just chipping in, so there was a real two-way going on.'

'It has lifted staff morale to see such an increase in numbers. They are more enthusiastic about the benefits of parental involvement.'

Parents

Schools often reported getting thank you letters after the workshop and there were many positive evaluation comments made by families.

'All parents enjoyed the session. We had to send them home at 11 a.m. I'm sure they would have stayed much longer.'

'The workshop was a great success, children and parents, teachers and the community librarian all enjoyed the morning. Photographs illustrate the high level of involvement by everyone.'

'Very calm atmosphere, everyone very absorbed and busy working together.'

'Parents suggested having one a month but I don't think we can. It would be like having Christmas every month.'

'One family worked shifts, so one came when the other one had to go.'

'Parents enjoyed the opportunity to see the teacher for an extended time – even if not talking to them directly, seeing how they related to the children.'

Other aims were to increase the involvement of parents in literacy and maths activities at home and to increase their understanding of learning at school. Workshop records demonstrated the ways in which both of these were being promoted.

(i) Activity at home
'Played commercially-produced games together. Looked at home-made games ideas and produced their own set of games to take home.'
   'Highlighting the importance of continued shared reading with KS 2.'
   'Before work went home but little was returned with little evidence of parents being involved.'
   'Talked about reading environmental print.'
   'Emphasis on fun way to practice number bonds and times tables at home.'

In 73 per cent of the schools staff reported that there had been an identifiable increase in educational activity in the home as a result of INSPIRE activities. The remaining 17 per cent did not feel that they had adequate mechanisms for telling whether or not this was so.

(ii) Understanding learning in the classroom
'Very useful for parents to have seen how children's writing develops.'
   'Showed parents and children our new maths games lending library.'
   'To make a storybook with their child focusing on beginning, middle and end.'
   'To make whole word and phonic games.'
   'Parents would now know what a number-line was and about letter formation.'
   'School and parents now have a shared understanding of approaches to literacy.'

In 88 per cent of the schools there had been an identifiable increase in parental understanding of the child's learning in the classroom as a direct result of INSPIRE activities; the remaining 12 per cent felt unable to check how far this was true.

The aim of raising achievement in literacy and maths was evaluated at two levels: at the level of day to day learning objectives and over a longer period. Involving parents in a joint activity with the children and then in reinforcing the learning at home was felt to bring greater success than when teachers worked alone with the children in the classroom. For example in one school, the children were assessed on knowledge of 'key words' before the workshop and three weeks after the workshop. Every child achieved 100 per cent in tests afterwards on their own selected words.

In the survey, schools were asked to assess the extent to which INSPIRE has led to longer-term raised attainment in literacy and maths. Sixty-one per cent reported that achievement had increased; the others felt that it was either too early in the INSPIRE process to tell, or that attainment was raised, but that this was due to such a complex mix of developments in the school that they could not separate out the specific effect of INSPIRE.

Other effects of the INSPIRE activity

Rebuilding parent/school relationships

At one school a couple had not been into the school for two years because of the exclusion of their older child. They had not been on speaking terms with the head teacher, but they spent much of the workshop morning talking to him. At another school, a parent had been banned from the premises for aggressive behaviour, but took their first step back into school through the workshop and the experience was very positive.

The numbers of parents completing evaluation forms surprised some schools. One was particularly surprised that on sending them home after forgetting to give them out at the workshop, so many were completed, quite fully, and returned.

Effect on the child's motivation/self-esteem

'The children were so proud (of their board games that they made); they had taken huge care with them.'

'During the break the children were asking to go inside and do some more.'

'Lots of parents commented on their child's attitude to work.'

One teacher described a child normally with a very poor concentration span who became completely engrossed, took his work home to finish with Mom and Dad and was so proud of himself.

One school, that specifically focuses on including children with special needs, had three children with behaviour difficulties in the workshop. The teacher commented on her delight and surprise at how well they all worked; that they remarkably stayed on task for the whole hour.

Effect on parent–child relationship

Feedback from parents at several schools was that it was an opportunity to spend quality time with their children.

'Saw parents talking to children in a way they don't usually.'

'One child had a tantrum and did not want the mother there. It was useful for the parent to see how the teacher dealt with him because he has tantrums a lot at home.'

Effect on the whole school

One school wrote: 'Positive responses were noticed in the atmosphere of the whole school.'

Referring to INSPIRE, one school said, 'It has made the school a community.'

More than one pair of separate Infant and Junior Schools were brought closer together through INSPIRE. One of them observed that they would be better coordinating, so that their workshops did not clash and take parents away from each other.

Several teachers reported improved parent evenings. One in particular said at a review session that he had had the best parents evening he had ever had in ten years.

A final positive outcome was that 'it is great PR for the school. It is part and parcel of a growing good reputation for the school; an important positive experience for all involved.'

Recurring phrases from individual schools have been identified and these have been packaged to represent the 'flavour' of what most schools were describing, using the schools' own words. Before INSPIRE, schools were describing their situations as follows.

Parental involvement was limited to general support around particular events (assemblies, open days), especially when their own child was involved. Contact around classroom practice was negligible. We saw the same small core of parents all the time; the same few attended everything, but the majority did not feel the need to come into school except when there was a problem. When they came in fault-finding, they could often be quite aggressive. We have always tried to make parents welcome and we work hard at it, but they do not always take up the opportunities. Parents' courses and parents' meetings have been tried – but little real take-up. There was a parents' group but numbers have dwindled to three or four. Others can be relied on for additional help when asked. Maybe the parents lack confidence to come in and there are not too many structured opportunities other than assemblies. There is more interest from the Infant parents than from the Juniors. Overall, contact with parents has been identified as a cause for concern.

After beginning their involvement with INSPIRE, the schools were describing their situation in the following terms:

Parental contact is now much more positive, informed, enthusiastic and demanding. There is a friendlier atmosphere between staff and parents. Both feel able to chat to each other informally. There is an enthusiasm on both sides. Parents are now looking for the next opportunities to be involved. More parents help out in the classroom; more parents are realistic about their expectations of school and feedback from the recent OFSTED parents meeting indicates a shared understanding and partnership.

Parents feel more able to come into school and ask questions about the work their child is doing. They are asking for information around the curriculum areas their child is following at the moment, and asking about ways in which they can help their children. Being more connected with the classroom, they feel able to become more involved in their child's work. The parents inform the teacher about work done at home. Those parents who were already involved are showing more interest in maths and are getting more involved in the work of their older children.

The school's approach is now more clearly planned and keeps a focus on the child's learning. Now that the majority of parents are involved we are able to target a much smaller number of parents with whom we are trying to work – making it feel much more manageable. Our work with parents overall has much more depth to it now.

Position of INSPIRE in the city framework

INSPIRE fits both into a cross-departmental city strategy for increasing family involvement in literacy and into the Education Department strategy for involving parents and communities with schools. It is also part of the corporate city approach to Lifelong Learning.

The cross-departmental family literacy group consists of representatives of various sections of the Education Department, Schools Advisory and Support Service, Pupil and School Support, and Pre-School Workers, and senior staff of the library service and the city Adult Education Service. The group came together to coordinate the many separate initiatives that were emerging through different departments and individual settings, and to combine our efforts in order to have a greater effect with families across the whole city. The group has developed an agreed Framework of Activities that we each promote and support in our own spheres of work and an action plan for encouraging the development of each strand and the joining up of services where appropriate.

The Framework of Activities includes family workshops (mostly through INSPIRE), information leaflets, tapes and videos, book loan schemes, book gifts (including Bookstart, see Chapter 8 by Wade and Moore), home activity packs, family activities (mostly in libraries) and Family Literacy. There is then a whole subgroup of activities targeted at Under-Fives, which also include, story-telling and book-sharing in the community, including health centres, 'Shopping to Read' (environmental print), 'Words on Wheels' (a library bus for under-fives), the promotion of rhyme, particularly Nursery Rhymes. Our aim is to encourage the availability of these activities to all families across the city.

Again, these activities can be found individually in many places across the country but in Birmingham these simple, effective strategies have become part of a joined-up plan, where different experiences for parents and families can build on each other with the purpose of increasing effectiveness for those involved. The most developed example of partnership working is the Family Literacy Programme. INSPIRE workshops are held as important precursors to these more intensive courses, bringing parents in and giving opportunities for the different partner providers to make contact and start to get to know the families.

Family literacy

This has been funded for the last three years through the Standards Fund, based on the Basic Skills Agency pilot model. The school, local library and local Adult Education Service, together with members of the Central group described above, work together in joint training, planning, monitoring and evaluating, as well as delivering, the 9–13-week courses. These are very different from INSPIRE activities. They target groups of ten Year 4 families based on specific literacy needs of those children and parents. They are intensive programmes where children and parents work separately for four hours and together for two hours each week. The aims are similar to those of INSPIRE in that they aim to improve attainment in literacy, home–school partnerships, and increase the amount of support available from home; but they also more specifically focus on the literacy needs of the parents.

As with the nationally researched programmes (Brooks *et al.* 1996) these courses in Birmingham have shown considerable success in the targeted outcomes. Achievements were clearly made in all areas for a majority of the families involved.

In 1997/8, 48 families were involved. There was a retention rate on the programme of 90 per cent. Over the two to three months, more than 75 per cent of children improved their reading ages from between four months and three years and there were many qualitative outcomes recorded.

Lifelong learning

Involving all members of a family in learning both together and separately helps to raise the status of education in a community. This in turn increases educational aspirations and expectations, increases children's motivation to learn and improves family support for children's learning. This has been demonstrated by many parent partnership projects throughout the country over the last decade.

A major difficulty has always been how to motivate parents to take the first step. As one such project in Birmingham began to fade, a school wrote, 'several courses had been organised with almost no take up. Parents signed up, made the right noises but never attended.'

Gillian Pugh in her three-year study of parental involvement in preschool services (Pugh 1989, page 10) wrote that 'few parents in the centres studied would have had the confidence to put themselves forward for the management committee had they not first participated in and been supported by groups and other activities in the schools or groups their child attended.'

INSPIRE has fulfilled this function for almost all aspects of parental involvement with schools. Even one workshop has put large numbers of parents at their ease in schools and with school staff. Certainly, as they attend one workshop after another for each of their children, they grow in confidence and more readily take up opportunities for involvement. This might be in school as volunteers, as governors, at meetings or on courses. So long as other barriers to participation are removed – lack of childcare, high costs, poor timing; the opportunities are at least initially at the school; and the parents continue to feel welcome, comfortable and valued they will go from strength to strength and one opportunity to another.

Veronica McGivney (1999) gave various case studies of this sort of progression into lifelong learning that began with INSPIRE workshops at two Birmingham Primary Schools. Parents became involved with computer courses, First Aid, English and/or Maths courses for themselves, Aromatherapy, Access to Classroom Assistants courses and NVQ Childcare as well as Employment and Training Guidance sessions. These were provided in community rooms at the schools as a partnership with the local Community Project, the Economic Development Department and local Adult Education Service and a Further Education College.

However, for the greatest effect, this must be treated quite sensitively. The workshops must be valued in their own right, and be appreciated for what they are – opportunities for parents, teachers and children to work together in partnership, for the sake of the school child. They should not be treated primarily as a stepping stone to somewhere else, as further education providers may be tempted to do. This is supported by Gillian Pugh when she wrote in her study (1989, page 12) that we need to, 'enable parents to develop at their own pace and not be rushed into activities before they are ready.' Parents must feel comfortable with just coming to the workshop and enjoy working with the school.

Summary

INSPIRE has made a huge difference to the involvement of parents and families in many Birmingham schools. The potential for a stronger partnership between home and school has thus been unleashed and it has broken through what one Birmingham governor described as 'the glass door'. It has also clearly demonstrated the positive contribution that parents can make to schools and to children's learning.

The Government's recent Excellence in Cities report (1999, page 6) states, 'We need to enable families to support their children, wherever possible providing backing and motivation – for example through home–school agreements, better information to parents, and family literacy.'

A few secondary schools are trialling ways of using INSPIRE workshops in their efforts to involve parents, particularly where it is well established in the feeder primary schools. Time will tell whether the exact model will work here, but certainly the principles that have been learnt will assist their effectiveness.

It remains the case that it should be the goal of all schools 'to enable every member of their community to taste the nectar of success...It should not however be a privilege for an elite; it should be the characteristic of the development of all our citizens.' (Brighouse and Tomlinson 1991, page 3).

Only little progress can be made in this until we change expectations and engage parents and schools equally with each other. We no longer have time only to build this up slowly with a few families at a time, we need strategies that can have an immediate impact on many and turn the situation around. In many Birmingham schools this has worked through INSPIRE.

References

Brighouse, T. and Tomlinson, J. (1991) *Successful Schools. Education and Training Paper No. 4*. London: Institute for Public Policy Research.

Brooks, G. *et al.* (1996) *Family Literacy Works*. London: Basic Skills Agency.

Central Advisory Committee for Education (1967) *Children and their Primary Schools* (The Plowden Report). London: HMSO.

Department of Education and Science (1975) *A Language for Life* (The Bullock Report). London: HMSO.

DfEE (1998) *The National Literacy Strategy, Framework for Teaching*. London: DfEE.

DfEE (1999) *Home–school Agreements Guidance for Schools*. London: DfEE.

Griffiths, A. and Hamilton, D. (1984) *Parent, Teacher, Child: Working together in children's learning*. London: Methuen.

McClelland, N. (ed.) (1997) *Building a Literate Nation*. London: Trentham Books.

McGivney, V. (1999) *Informal Learning in the Community*. London: National Institute of Adult Continuing Education.

Moser, C. (1999) *A Fresh Start; Basic skills for adults*. London: DfEE.

Pugh, G. (1989) 'Pre-school Services: Is Partnership Possible?', in Wolfendale, S. (ed.) *Parental Involvement: Developing Networks Between Home, School and Community*. London: Cassell Educational.

Tomlinson, S. (1991) *Teachers and Parents, Home–school Partnerships. Education and Training Paper No. 7*. London: Institute for Public Policy Research.

Chapter 5

An LEA perspective on parental involvement*

Sue Barnes

This chapter seeks to explore the very specific experience of one new unitary authority in achieving greater involvement of parents in their own education and their children's learning. It describes a two-year programme undertaken, the issues this work has raised and a discussion of the way forward for the authority over the next three years.

The author is a School Improvement Adviser whose additional responsibility includes Family and Community Education. The perspective on parental involvement, including family learning is in terms of how this dimension impinges on school improvement and the raising achievement agenda in schools. The perspective is therefore one which is constrained but offered as a way of sharing our learning with the wider education community.

Background information

This city-based authority became unitary in April 1997. The Director of Education, when establishing the small advisory team in the Quality and Development Branch of the Education Department, was clear from the outset that he wanted a post which included Family Education. At that time it was a unique post; one which two years on, obviously had a lot of foresight. Its creation, therefore, established an agenda of the perceived importance and direction of parental involvement and in raising educational achievement and, in highlighting the importance of the three-way partnership between home, pupil and school and lifelong learning.

In 1997, the new LEA found itself very near the bottom of the national league tables at Key Stages 1 and 2 and near the bottom for Key Stage 3. Key Stage 4 results which, although well below national averages, showed that schools, particularly those with high ethnic

---

* The views expressed in this chapter are those of the author in a personal context and not those of Leicester LEA or Council.

populations, were achieving. The authority had inherited over 20 schools which were on Special Measures or Serious Weaknesses. It also had more than a quarter of its schools still to be inspected by OFSTED in the final year of the first round of inspections. As these inspections took place and their results were analysed, there has been increasing acknowledgement of parental involvement as being significant.

The growing bank of socio-economic data has gradually become more easily available and accessible to elected members and officers, through the development of new technologies. It showed a clear relationship between disadvantage, disaffection and low educational achievement of both adults and children. This, coupled with information on poor health indicators and unemployment levels, showed a correlation with those school catchments with the lowest achievement data and the poorest OFSTED results. As a now data-rich authority able to use this information and able to overlay learning participant data, the targeting of projects and initiatives is always against this background.

The authority had also inherited a long-standing and proud tradition of a school-based Community Education Service. This was complemented in certain of the most disadvantaged communities by freestanding Community Education projects, born in previous funding regimes from the 'Inner Area Programme of Urban Regeneration'. High quality parent and family work was often a feature of the 'under-fives' work being undertaken. The Community Education Service would have been a natural place to look for extending work and financial support to schools wanting to undertake developmental work with parents. However, in reality, the Service, although very well resourced financially, had an expensive fixed staffing structure out of balance with its flexible resource structure because of years of funding cuts. This meant that the Service was unable to change to meet fast growing and different agendas. But it did have good practice to draw on.

There was also inequality of school-based community provision across the city, with 80 per cent of secondary schools and 10 per cent of primary schools resourced as community schools. This inequality was further compounded by Section 11, now Ethnic Minority Achievement Grant (EMAG) funding, which had provided a talented and effective work force of home–school liaison workers and coordinators. These were often also the primary schools with community designation. At the onset of unitary status, therefore, resources to support parental involvement schemes were polarised to primary schools which had a high ethnic minority population. There was only one very small community primary school, struggling to bring in adult learners, in the southern half of the city with its traditionally disadvantaged white outer ring council estates.

As is often the case with any new authority, there was a need to rationalise its current use of financial resources. Within the first few months, the LEA prepared to conduct a review of all its education provision systems. This started with a Secondary Education Review, to address falling rolls and surplus places. This has resulted in the closure of six secondary schools in the most disadvantaged areas of the City. Five of these were Community Colleges. This review was closely followed by a Special Schools Review. The Community Education and the Primary School Review were announced together and are running concurrently. The implementation date for the Community Education Review is scheduled for early 2001. The Primary Review is ongoing. Systems and structures were therefore unlikely to be changed within the first two years to release new funding possibilities.

A personal perspective

My background, first as a primary trained teacher and then as an Adult Basic Education worker, meant I had often been in contact with parents who were being described by some schools as 'not caring' or 'not interested' in the education their children were receiving. More worrying was a feeling expressed in some schools by staff, that many of their parents didn't want to be involved. This was compounded by anti-parental feeling by staff in quite a number of schools.

The reality I had witnessed from those parents who had become my adult basic skills students, was that the life challenges facing some parents, linked to their own educational experiences, had left them lacking in confidence in an educational setting, often feeling very threatened and inadequate when dealing with any type of authority. Some parents regularly met this challenge with aggression and some, faced with the dilemma of choice, felt it better to leave the education of their children to 'the professional', while they tackled some of the other difficulties facing their families. Parents frequently felt that they had little rapport with their children's teachers. Although many schools were using the term 'partner' or 'partnership', in reality the power was still vested with the teachers and not the parents. There were also, however, examples of good practice in a number of schools which had long-standing sound and innovative work with parents. This was, however, contrasted by a large number of schools with no parental involvement at all other than that required by statute.

As a School Improvement Adviser with a case-load of schools, I had no additional staffing and no budget for the developmental aspects of the post. The challenge in the first instance was how to make an impact on this situation quickly and bring about a culture change.

The first ally was the then new Labour Government. The words in the White Paper *Excellence in Schools,* in Chapter 6, of referring to parents as the 'first and most important educators' and later as 'co-educators of their children', prefaced every speech I made. The second message constantly used was the 15–85 per cent split between 'in school' and 'out of school' learning opportunities available to pupils. I quickly found I had other allies in head teachers, early years educators, librarians and community education staff, many of whom were keen to become more able to effectively involve parents.

A much more daunting task, however, was to start to convince senior managers and colleagues that involving parents was not just about paying lip service, that getting parents involved was not only a good idea, but that it would contribute significantly in the long term to the raising achievement agenda.

Two years on it's difficult to realise that this was the scenario. The whole national inclusion movement, of course, has helped to shape current thinking too.

The pace of change

The last two years have been a time of rapid movement brought about by changes not only in the developing strategy of the LEA to bring about school improvement and raise standards but also against a backdrop of emerging and developing policies and approaches of the new Labour Government's education strategy. But the pace of change and the plethora of national initiatives to which schools and the LEA have had to respond has meant that 'please include and inform the parents' has had to be a constant and repetitive cry. In the social inclusion agenda, raising achievement has always been a key theme, but so too has the acknowledgement and promotion of the role which adults and parents could and should play. Work to ensure greater parental involvement in education has had to be flexible to accommodate all this change. At times it has had to be both proactive and reactive.

Getting started

Baseline data on parental aspects in the LEA provided by the OFSTED performance and assessment data (PANDA), showed that on all the parental indicators, its schools were doing reasonably well compared to its benchmark group; but that compared to national norms the Authority was behind on every other indicator. It also showed that schools which had striven to involve parents were often more successful than those which had not.

There was, however, no detailed data or evidence of where current practice was in schools in the city. I therefore started by devising a simple questionnaire to give some baseline audit data. It was sent out to all schools within a month of arriving in post. It was hoped that this would also signal clearly the areas in which the Education Department wanted to develop good parental involvement practice. Schools were asked questions about the number of parents currently working or volunteering in school, arrangements for induction into school, home visiting, attendance at parents evenings, whether or not the school had a policy on home–school relations or on parental involvement, whether the school had any experience of projects or programmes which promoted parental involvement together with any evidence of their impact, whether the school ran any out-of-school activities, transition arrangements and strategies from one stage of education to another and whether the school had plans to, or was interested in, developing these areas of work.

There was an incomplete data return, despite sending out the questionnaire twice and publishing the findings in the first newsletter of the department. But the return was substantial enough to give pointers as to where to start work. Only six schools out of 121 had policies specifically on parental involvement although a higher number indicated that there was a parental dimension in a number of their whole–school policies. Only a small percentage of schools had undertaken any projects working specifically with parents but many more said they were interested in developing this area of their work. Very few parents were involved in schools as volunteers although schools indicated that they had tried, often unsuccessfully, to get them involved.

Sometimes an absence of comments on report forms was taken to mean disinterest, whereas the problem might be a lack of confidence. The following are examples of a teacher and a parent talking about the same incident:

'I sent out twenty-nine reports last week. Only four of them had parents' comments on when they were returned'. (teacher)

'I got his report the other day, I didn't write anything on it, well you don't like to, do you, when you can't spell very well and were hopeless at school and you know a teacher is going to read it'. (parent)

A two-year strategy

Against the above background and with the audit information, a six-strand approach to developing parental involvement and family education in the first two years was discussed with senior managers, actioned and embarked upon. City-wide strategy writing and policy development, in this area as with many others, was left as 'we hit the ground running' to try to make an impact on school standards and was left until the climate was right at a later date. In the first instance a very pragmatic approach was taken to raising the profile of parental education and involvement.

The approach was to:
(i) Develop *partnership working* wherever possible so as to synergise capacity, expertise and resources in order to be as proactive as possible.
(ii) Develop *two or three city-wide projects* grounded within the raising achievement strategy of the Education Department which would demonstrate the difference the involvement of parents could make. These would also serve as a vehicle for training for school staff to become more confident to work with adults. (These projects are described later in the text and are called 'Share', 'Keeping Up with the Kids' and 'Moving on Up'.)
(iii) *Promote the parental involvement* opportunities in any initiative the Education Department undertook.
(iv) Seek where possible to *support any individual school programme*, intervention strategy or project which promoted parental involvement.
(v) To be proactive in *sharing information and good practice* through regular communication by means of departmental newsletters, network groups, seminars, workshops, conferences and NQT and governor training that emphasised the importance of parental involvement.
(vi) Seek to apply for *additional funding* for parental involvement projects.

Outcomes

• Partnership working

This strand has successfully forged partnership between other council departments, other education providers including FE and HE, voluntary agencies and with the Careers and Guidance Service, the Training and Enterprise Council (TEC) and, to a lesser extent, with business. Within each individual project partnership arrangement, it has been key from the start, planning and working together, to monitor progress and to evaluate outcomes which satisfied the individual aims and targets of each individual organisation or institution. Each organisation therefore agreed a common agenda and joint outcomes but also each had its own project outcomes to work towards achieving. The introduction of other 'agencies' into schools has affected the quality of projects worked on and has provided other opportunities and openings which parents have been able to access. Lasting relationships and different projects have arisen in the schools as a result. This partnership working has therefore had the added value of starting to move some schools away from being 'a school in the community' to being a 'community' school offering access to a range of services. In turn, parents have been able to talk face to face with service providers.

For all the literacy-based projects, the Adult Basic Education Service and the Library Service have worked together, often additionally funded through the TEC. Here, the synergy has resulted not only in developing parents' own literacy needs but has also been used to introduce parents to an FE College environment, to provide adult education facilitators in school to model good adult education practice and also to promote the use of the Library Service.

Over two years, the partnership with the FE College has seen the continuance of the 'Parents as Partners in...' (reading or maths or learning)' courses in a number of schools, the development of a very successful model for the Standards Fund Family Literacy programme also in partnership with the Library Service and the Special Needs Teaching Service. The Standards Fund Summer Literacy and Numeracy School programmes were also used as an opportunity to provide sessions for parents as well as children. Partnership in this scheme included local businesses as sponsors, 'Leicester Mercury, Newspapers in Education' Project, The Education Welfare Service and the Speakeasy Theatre Company. Partnership working has therefore proved to be very fruitful and has enabled schools to get to know other services and agencies and to access workers in others who have been able to bring in additional resources and personnel.

• *Three city-wide parental involvement projects*
In August 1997, the LEA through a 'by chance' contact had secured a place on the Community Education Development Centre Share programme, as it started the second year of its National Demonstration Project. It was quickly realised that this project, described in Chapter 9 of this book, offered the opportunity to provide a framework and mechanism to be able to work with schools on parental involvement in the basic skills curriculum and raising standards. It would also provide resources and a framework for developing expertise in working with adults for classroom based teachers through a substantial training programme. Looking for volunteer schools to take

part in the Share programme showed the potential interest in schools for working with 'off the shelf' materials. This project has again been worked in partnership with the Adult Basic Education Service. Each project school has had their own ABE tutor attached to them for a term. This project now, two years later, will be operating in 25 schools and has done much to carry parental work forward both in schools and in the city as a whole. In terms of its impact on raising standards, evaluation shows that no Share child has achieved less than that predicted for them, that parents have become more involved in their children's learning and that the quality of learning in the home has increased. Currently parents drawn into school originally through Share are working as ancillaries, governors, toy library leaders and informed and trained classroom volunteers, and are actively promoting school based adult learning programmes to friends and family.

> 'It has given me a lot more confidence in myself and made me realise that I can achieve something for myself and that I am able to come up with ideas.'

> 'I have had a great time and made some new friends and had a great time learning how to help my boy.'

> 'I always said I would never go back to school but now I wish I could start all over again.'

> (Share parents)

The second project strand developed across the City was that of Family Literacy. Research showed that the development of *adult/family literacy programmes* which also showed parents how to support their children's learning were extremely beneficial. This type of initiative would complement the obvious first priority for the LEA of raising literacy achievement at Key Stage 1 and 2 and also of raising achievement of adult literacy – a huge issue for this authority. Evaluation comments such as:

> 'I'd do it all again if I could' (parent).

> 'It's been brilliant. I never thought I could achieve something like this' (a parent on receipt of her first Open College accredited certificate), 'I'm going to do a maths course next.'

and

> 'He's changed from a child who wouldn't to a child who can... 'I've been amazed at just how much progress he's [son] made in such a short time and how much we've talked at home.'

show the lasting change brought about by this type of intervention.

Throughout the two years this partnership has developed and proved very fruitful. It has worked with over 150 parents in Share and 50 parents in the Family Literacy projects.

The third city-wide project, called 'Moving on Up', was a transition project between the primary and secondary phase of education. Originally the funding was given by the Health Authority through Community Service Volunteers (CSV) for adults who had lost confidence by being at home to volunteer to work in secondary schools. The project funding was for two years and was fairly substantial. After several weeks of negotiation, the 'Moving on Up' project was agreed. Its design was to attract adults into the primary school to receive training to support and befriend vulnerable Year 6 children to help them in the classroom and also with transition to their new secondary school and to continue the support through the first half term whilst they settled into their new school.

In reality most of the adults recruited were also parents. The WEA supplied the accredited course 'Helping in Schools', the Adult Basic Education Service provided the day to day coordination and some of the training for the project, while the LEA provided additional training on how primary and secondary schools work. The Careers and Guidance Service provided workshops at the end of the course for participants to reflect on the transferable skills they had developed, to write a CV, and to give advice and guidance on progression routes and career opportunities. The Education Business Partnership based at the TEC provided the evaluation aspects of the course. Thirty parents have been through this programme with four gaining employment as ancillaries in schools and many more continuing to develop their own education through local community or adult education courses.

• Parental involvement education department initiatives

The advent of the National Literacy Strategy allowed another opportunity to promote parental involvement. The four-part parental strategy (see Figure 5.1) advocated in the National Literacy Framework is one which was promoted to all schools at the Literacy Conferences held in the summer of 1998. It was used as a medium to try to promote parental involvement in a structured way for schools.

Inform	Involve at school
Involve at home	Support

Figure 5.1

Information leaflets to send out to parents were written by the Education Department for schools to use with their parent body. A basic design and simple text was sent out on disk for schools to customise for their own context and use. The two literacy consultants also offered to go into schools to talk to parent groups invited into school to learn more about the literacy strategy and the Literacy Hour. Link advisers encouraged schools to put on literacy hour demonstrations and taster sessions. A recent survey showed that over 3,000 parents have been involved in information meetings and workshops.

However, the diverse ethnic language base of the city meant that there was also a need to be proactive to inform parents of the literacy hour in their own community language. There were a number of reasons for this. There was a realistic fear that some of the ethnic communities would see themselves as being targeted by this strategy rather than the strategy being a national initiative. Secondly there is no word in many of the ethnic community languages spoken which is the equivalent of 'literacy'. To help to address these issues a collaborative project between four schools, the Multicultural Education Service and the University of Leicester, School of Education funded by the Education Department, the TEC and the Leicestershire Careers and Guidance Service was set up. Its purpose was to produce a short promotional video which had four aims:

(i)   a definition of literacy;
(ii) a description of the purpose of the National Literacy Strategy;
(iii) the literacy hour in school;
(iv) a celebration of what parents already did in the home which supported the development of literacy and ideas about how they could help further.

The video will be available in five community languages. Schools will be able to buy copies for their parents to borrow to watch at home. As schools move on to focus on the Numeracy Strategy this year, it will also act as a resource for new parents to the school and to the country.

The LEA in partnership with the Adult Basic Education Service saw the opportunity presented through the National Literacy Strategy of informing parents and addressing their own literacy needs. An innovative project called 'Keeping up with the Kids' was designed and funding applied for to the FEFC and the Basic Skills Agency. Parents were recruited to come into schools for a 20-hour course, spread over five weeks, to learn about the literacy hour through experiencing it at an adult level and addressing some of their own literacy needs at the same time. At the end of a one year programme more than 220 parents have been involved in 39 schools. A pilot project 'Keeping up with the Kids – Maths' is currently being trialled in three schools and there is a waiting list of schools wanting to benefit from the initiative.

Throughout this period the Authority has also been involved in bidding for and being given some of the government national innovative programmes.

Within the first few months, bidding for an Early Excellence Centre was underway. This was an innovative bid based on a family involvement programme which worked with families of children from 0–5 to give them the best start at school. It was based on a disadvantaged council estate, had been running for about six months and was starting to show its potential for change. The bid was finally turned down because there was too much adult work in the programme. However, a very similar model has now been accepted as the Sure Start bid.

The authority began work on bidding for an Education Action Zone (EAZ) in March 1998. Family and parental education were a prominent feature in one of its strands. This successful application for an EAZ centred on the southern ring of four council estates and 21 schools. Currently six parent link workers are each assigned to geographical areas of the zone to work with schools to try to break down some of the barriers between home and school. The idea of the kite mark of 'The Welcoming School' is also being developed.

One of these estates was also selected for New Deal for Communities status. An adjoining estate is the focus for a 12 million pound bid for Single Regeneration Funding. Parent and family education are again prominent features.

There is a partnership and interagency working in all these initiatives. The education theme is always to raise standards of achievement but there is now a growing awareness about the role of family education, parenting skills education and the development of activities to promote adult literacy and their link to potential community regeneration activity. The Lifelong Learning Development Plan and the Lifelong Strategic Partnerships are now also starting to develop work which involves parents at a number of levels. Ongoing national initiatives such as home–school agreements, homework and study support have also given a focus to help schools to include parents in their particular context!

• *Support any individual school programme, intervention strategy or project which promoted parental involvement.*
A number of schools have wanted to be proactive in finding innovative ways to involve parents and have looked to the Education Department for support. The task here, despite the context of the

school, is to make sure that the 'climate' is right inside the school and that the parental initiative is clearly linked to a school development priority; that projects have clear and realistic targets and outcomes and that monitoring and evaluation systems are in place.

• *Regular communication to share information and good practice*
Regular communication and information in a variety of formats have been essential in order to promote the importance of parental involvement and to share evaluation and impact. The work was launched with a city-wide conference. Training courses and workshops have followed. Case studies are spoken about at network meetings and projects are described in the Education Department newsletter. The local newspaper will often follow a personal success story which has been highlighted in a regular weekly education feature called 'Learning Life'.

There has also been a need to keep adviser colleagues up to date and informed about new and ongoing projects in order that they can both understand the purpose and carry the message to the schools for which they have responsibility. Where possible, colleagues have been supported to help their schools with the work, so that expertise is shared and not vested with one worker. It has been important, too, that this work has been reported to elected members and to the City Literacy and Numeracy Steering Group, a wide-ranging multiagency task group. All parental work is reported through this group in an annual report to members. The work is therefore grounded in the school improvement agenda.

Parental involvement work and family learning which have been identified as priorities in the Education Development Plan are also priorities for literacy, numeracy, special educational needs and for increasing participation.

• *Additional funding for parental involvement projects*
Short-term funding has, over the course of the two years, been found to work on many of the projects. A rich source of this has come about as a result of partnership work. Funding is often easier to come by if there are several sponsors. Once the first sponsor is committed the others will follow. A creative project design which allows for all the funders' objectives to be met is all that is needed!

Current developments

Schools are beginning to gather evidence on the impact of this area of work and are able to make judgements about its potential value-added on a range of indicators which all ultimately impact on school standards. A quote from a Section 3 HMI report for a school being removed from Special Measures says: 'Links with parents have been considerably strengthened. For example, the family literacy project is helping parents improve their children's learning.'

Two years on, there are a number of issues which are emerging and which will need to be addressed if the development of this area of work is to reflect its true potential:

- The work can be marginalised because it is not high profile and adequately resourced. It is usually underfunded and in times of constraints on budget this can be one of the first areas to be cut in a school. The Authority will have to find a secure and sustainable resourcing commitment if the work is to really develop.
- The strategy for school improvement will need to include the out-of-school curriculum described in its broadest sense and including parent involvement. Education and regeneration policy-makers will need to be clear about the importance of both and the dynamics of the relationship between the two.
- School-based community work will need extra resourcing if it is to be found in all schools as a matter of course.
- There need to be many more funded staff development opportunities if a school is to become reliant on its own staff to deliver parent education through its own staffing resources. This developing expertise needs to be recognised through an appropriate accreditation and quality assurance system.

The way forward

Although the six strands outlined above had specific work and initiatives attached to them, in reality those strands have become interwoven in most of the developmental projects undertaken. The outcomes for each have often overlapped. The strands, rather than remaining distinct, have now became key features of most of the work. The involvement of parents is obviously the constant factor in all the work undertaken but the parents will be in differing roles. They can be categorised as work with:

- parents as clients for services including education;
- parents as active learners;
- parents as potential learners;
- parents as co-educators and role models;
- parents as a force for change.

Also, the focus of the work needs to reflect their different needs in those roles. Unless that happens, then the danger of any work undertaken in the future will be seen to be trying to only attract parents who appear to be challenged by their role of being a 'good enough' parent. Having the option and the entitlement and the access to being involved in learning, schooling and adult education in the way that is best for each individual parent and family needs to become the entitlement for all. This will not come about by chance, it must be strategically planned and resourced. For the particular city in question, this will come about through the Lifelong Learning Development Plan where family education in its widest sense will be developed as a strategy for the city. This will ultimately be resourced through the Standard Spending Allowance (SSA) of the Council, providing that in the new climate of the post-16 White Paper *Learning to Succeed* the local authority retains its statutory duty to secure provision for adults.

As part of the vision for a new city authority, lifelong learning is now becoming a reality in its working practices, based on the foundations of raising standards and improving the quality of life for participants. Much has been achieved in a relatively short time, but if we are to see longer-term benefits, strategic planning and additional resources for family learning will need to be secured and sustained to make the long-term vision a reality. There remains much still to be done.

Chapter 6

The contribution of parents to school effectiveness: Newham's City Challenge Action for Achievement Project

Bala Bawa

This chapter describes a specific initiative to raise children's educational achievement by enhancing parental involvement within an urban, inner city area, the London Borough of Newham in the East End of London. This account gives the background to Newham, details of the City Challenge Action for Achievement Project, project findings and outcomes and current initiatives.

Background

Newham is estimated to have a population of 234,000 and is one of the fastest growing areas of East London, with expanding housing developments and increasing birth rates. Rising school rolls make up one of the highest ratios in the country. It has the second highest level of ethnic minority residents in Britain, at 42.3 per cent, including a large number of refugees from a wide diversity of backgrounds. There is constant transition of the population entering and leaving the Borough, as well as relocation within Newham.

Newham is ranked as the second most deprived authority in the country, for example: unemployment at 11.2 per cent (June 1998); 41 per cent of the school rolls are eligible for free school meals; one in three residents are dependent on some form of benefit; 62.1 per cent of unemployed residents in the London East region have been unemployed for more than six months; the percentage of pupils gaining five or more GCSEs Grades A–C in Newham is 27.9 per cent and the proportion of residents with no qualifications (21.1 per cent) is markedly higher than the average for Greater London (12.4 per cent).

A number of policies were formulated during the 1980s to try to combat the underachievement (Wolfendale 1996). A strong feature still continues to be the range of community involvement and community based initiatives through Newham's Community Education and Youth Service. The Service now operates in four areas in the Borough, coordinating and managing numerous initiatives for adults, youth and schools.

The Hegarty Report (Hegarty 1989) resulting from Newham Council and the LEA's independent inquiry into educational achievement within the Borough recommended that the LEA should foster home–school communication at all levels and that home–school work should assume greater importance (Wolfendale 1996).

The Parents in Partnership policy was adopted by the Education Committee in 1993, resulting from consultation between schools, parents and parent workers within education. Newham was also the first LEA to have a parent representative on its Education Committee, now a requirement within the 1998 Education Act.

In targeting the poverty and underachievement in Newham several sources of external funding have been helpful. These include: Section 11; Urban Aid programme; Docklands PACT; DfEE/GEST (Grants for Education and Training) Stratford City Challenge; Single Regeneration Budget (Green Street and Canning Town) and the Council/LEA grants.

Newham's Learning Community Strategy, launched in 1997, aims to develop an education culture in all communities and raise achievement by establishing a climate for learning within schools and a commitment to education in the wider community (Learning Community Progress Report 1999b).

The objectives in relation to this aim are to:

- raise expectations among young people and adults as to levels of educational achievement that they can attain;
- secure active support in all communities for strategies designed to raise levels of achievement of children, young people and adults;
- increase the motivation of, and participation by, children in the education and learning process by developing and marketing a range of additional educational opportunities;
- build local partnerships that promote the learning community strategy.

Newham's Education Action Zone (EAZ), in the south west of the Borough, set up in 1998, has enabled the LEA to pilot and develop initiatives for raising educational achievement. The EAZ Partnership consisting of schools, businesses and Newham Council will:

bring about radical improvements in the **education** of young people and adults in south-west Newham by harnessing the **enterprise** of professional educationalists, local communities and the business and voluntary sectors. Our aim is to achieve **excellence** in all the schools in the area and to develop systems for the rapid **exchange** of information about good practice both within the zone, nationally and internationally.

(Newham EAZ, Action Plan 1999 to 2001)

The City Challenge Action for Achievement Project

As project coordinator, this author will describe the Stratford City Challenge Action for Achievement Project, a five-year project with quantitative and qualitative targets focusing on raising achievement through enhancing parental involvement in the two nurseries, seven primary schools and one Special school in the designated area. (Bawa, Reports 1993–1997 and Wolfendale, Reports 1993-1998)

The project represented a major Government-funded initiative to regenerate certain inner city areas such as Stratford in Newham. The project enabled initiatives to be set up, developed and established over its five-year period (1993-8).

Throughout this period the project continued to enhance, complement and build upon existing resources and best practice models in the schools and where possible to incorporate good practice models into other schools.

The aims of the project were to:

- improve parental involvement in schools in order to boost achievement of children;
- contribute towards the development of local communities through increased adult participation at educational institutions;
- raise expectations of pupils, parents and teachers to fully optimise the environment changes planned, such as new housing, a new cinema, supporting local businesses and the general regeneration of the area.

The following specific targets were set over 5 years.

Quantitative targets
1. To effect an increase of 25 per cent attendance at parents events/evenings by the end of the five-year period in each school. (Individual figures collected at the start of year 1 as a baseline.)
2. To have achieved a 20 per cent improvement on 1991 Key Stage 1 SATs in English and Mathematics by the end of the five-year period; also an unspecified improvement in Key Stage 2 SATs dependent upon the outcome of first Key Stage 2 assessments.
3. To establish a steering group to manage the project during year 1.
4. To establish an area school governor forum by the end of year 1.
5. To establish a parent organisation in each school by the end of year 3.
6. To establish an area parent/governor forum by the end of year 4.
7. To establish parent newsletters in all schools by the end of year 3.
8. To have held a conference by the end of year 2.
9. To have published a booklet of good practice initiatives by the end of year 2.

Qualitative targets

1. To establish fully the LEA policy of 'partnership with parents' in all City Challenge schools.
2. To improve teacher, parent and pupil expectations during the course of the programme.
3. To show evidence of improved continuity of parental involvement between nursery/primary/secondary transition.
4. To develop systems of shared homework activities involving parents.
5. To establish a structure of training parental involvement for parents/governors and school staff.
6. To improve the participation of parents in adult education courses.
7. To establish firm links between parents organisations with the Parents Advice Centre (based at the Stratford Advice Centre), voluntary organisations and the City Challenge Forum.

For each school to genuinely take on board parental involvement, a policy in consultation with governors, parents and staff needed to be adopted. Schools were given copies of the LEA policy as a starting point, for consultation, in order to, either adopt the policy as it stands or to develop their own Parental Involvement policy in line with the LEA policy. This initial consultation provided an ideal opportunity for a dialogue with school staff, including each other as well as with parents and governors. Schools adopted different strategies for this consultation process, for example in one school:

- awareness raising using the LEA policy;
- working parties to formulate School Parental Involvement Policy;
- LEA policy accepted and an additional 'School Parental Involvement Policy', was written after staff meetings;
- both policies taken to governing body meeting, 2 March 1994;
- parents were informed;
- school staff already following guidelines on Parental Involvement;
- launch of policy;
- user-friendly leaflet, with children's illustrations, giving guidelines for working with children.

Project structure, organisation and monitoring

The project was managed by the project coordinator through the representative Steering Committee. The coordinator was responsible for monitoring the project, collecting data, providing support and training for school based staff as well as liaising with other projects. Management of the project at school level took place through each individual school's management structure. Each school identified a member of staff as a link teacher with special responsibility for developing parental involvement. The project coordinator supported the link teachers in developing the individual school action plan based on the overall project aims and targets.

Participating nursery, primary and special schools received funding for a set number of days each year to release link teachers from the timetable. Schools also received an allocation for further resource development of curriculum materials and specific training for governors/parents/teachers.

The link teachers devised strategies, building on initiatives started previously and establishing parental involvement. A planning and monitoring form was used to review, modify where necessary and show how the targets were met.

The project was monitored by the coordinator using a variety of the following methods.

- **Planning and monitoring forms** were completed by link teachers and forwarded to the coordinator. The returns gave details of initiatives developed during each term and indications of any issues that might need intervention, help or support by the coordinator or other relevant person/agency. This process enabled the coordinator to ensure that the project was progressing towards meeting the targets. It also enabled schools to carry out their own monitoring, using a standard format.
- **The Coordinator's monitoring visits** were used to support link teachers. They helped teachers to focus on targets and what had been, or needed to be, achieved, to ensure progression towards success. The planning and monitoring forms were used for this purpose also. Outcomes were agreed and recorded and a copy left with the link teacher.
- **Budget authorisation forms** were completed by schools and the spend authorised by the coordinator, giving an up to date account of spend by each school.
- **The Steering Committee** provided support and guidance to the project coordinator, conducting a termly review of progress, testing ideas and giving general direction.
- **Link teachers meetings** were held regularly each term, helping teachers to plan and review the progress and explore ways of moving forward. The meetings also enabled teachers to share good practice with each other, give mutual support on difficult issues and to work on the specific initiatives each year, such as leaflets for parents and conferences.
- **Informal feedback** from a number of individuals and agencies, including head teachers, other LEA workers, parents and the voluntary sector also helped to focus on individual issues.

- **External evaluation** by Professor Sheila Wolfendale, University of East London, working closely with the project staff. Sheila Wolfendale was approached to become the evaluator due to her long-standing involvement in a number of Newham initiatives and, most relevant, her local and national work and writings on parental involvement. It was agreed the evaluation brief would also include the role of 'critical friend'.

Project findings

In order to meet the first Qualitative target on increasing attendance, a range of different initiatives were developed by schools to increase attendance at parents evenings and other events. These included:

Parents' evenings supported by other activities, taking place at the same time:
- exhibitions
- book fair, to encourage parents to buy books for their children
- teachers encouraging parents to make appointments at other times also
- giving questionnaires to parents to see what they want
- showing videos of the children working and/or videos showing how parents can help their children to read
- introducing an appointment system.

Other parental involvement events included:
- setting up parents' room/area, involving parents in initial planning and organising appropriate activities
- making the parents' room a welcoming focal point for parents and enabling them to take up ownership
- organising talks, discussions and practical activities in identified areas, such as the curriculum, adult education, and social activities.

Table 6.1 gives the increase in attendance over four years.

As schools had different needs, link teachers required differentiated support in meeting the set targets, particularly where some teachers had still not endorsed these project targets. The evaluator points out:

Overall, positive enthusiasm was expressed for the aims of and involvement in the project, which is clearly establishing itself, in some schools more quickly than others.

whereas a few years ago, there was stated ambivalence towards parental involvement, now there is growing acceptance of parents' rights to involvement in education (via legislation) and the parental contribution towards their children's education (as demonstrated by many other similar projects elsewhere).

(Wolfendale, Annual Report 1994)

Table 6.1 (Bawa, Annual Report 1997)

School	(Baseline) 93/4	Attendance 94/5	Attendance 95/6	Attendance 96/7
N1	70%	96% average at extra events	95% average at extra events	97.8 extra events
N2	58%	65%	82% average at extra events	67% (+ other events)
P1	72%	55% PE (+ other events)	56% PE only	82% (+ other events)
P2	61%	59% PE (+ other events)	69% PE only	37% (+ other events)
P3	72%	73% PE (+ other events)	65% PE + other events	55% (+ other events)
P4	Data unavailable	64% PE (+ other events)	80% PE only	73% (+ other events)
P5	66%	73% PE (+ other events)	77% PE only	83%
P6	90%	84% PE (+ other events)	76% PE (100% in reality as all parents seen)	88% (+ all parents seen)
S1	Data unavailable	48%	79%	100% (termly objective meetings)

Key:
N = Nursery school   P = Primary school   S = Special school   PE = Parents evening

One of the evaluation exercises was the Parents Questionnaire. This confirmed the comprehensive range of activities they had been involved with, enjoyed and benefited from. Parents were also clear about how their children had gained. Some verbatim responses are given below:

'More time with my child.'
'I feel I have a clearer role.'
'I now understand what my child gets from Nursery Education.'
'I feel I have accomplished something.'
'Giving something back to the school.'

At the end of the first year the impact of the project was summed up by one of the link teachers:

'An immense impact…the parents feel the "school" as a whole is more approachable and feel so much more comfortable about coming into school and discussing concerns in a calmer manner…The parents room is a hive of activity…The amount of parents helping in school has increased.'

Standard Assessment Tasks (SATs) results at Key Stage 1 and Key Stage 2 were not possible to compare accurately as the criteria changed during the project. However, the increased awareness of parents showed expectations had increased and education appeared to be valued more. Parents became more interested and involved in homework, particularly in literacy and numeracy.

The wide range of members on the Steering Committee and Area Governor Forum were able to provide support, guidance, test ideas, and give general direction in moving the project forward.

The Parent Associations established in each school participated in activities such as fund-raising, homework clubs, supporting at school events such as concerts and assemblies. Newsletters were also set up for parents by parents with support from the head teacher or other staff.

The target of increasing expectations of parents, teachers and pupils links into all aspects of the project. Expectations constantly improved as teachers, parents and children became more aware of each others' potential. The coordinator worked closely with the external evaluator, to sample class teachers' views on working in partnership with parents, specifically to find out if expectations had improved during the project. Teachers' verbatim comments as detailed in the Wolfendale Annual Report 1995 include:

'expectations have been raised through development of consistent strategies.'

'in most instances better insight into child from parents raises expectations, and cooperation is more efficient.'

'it's good to see children attaining that potential when they are given extra support.'

'PACT [Parents and Children and Teachers] has been a real eye-opener – it's given me opportunities to learn something about children's competencies that I would not otherwise have known.'

'PACER' [Parents and Children Enjoy Reading] has made my expectations of the children who attend higher, in the school sessions.'

'children internalise that school is valued and important by the many important people in their lives.'

'the gain is on extension of education into the home, which is relevant to the child and parents.'

'raise self-esteem and confidence.'

'parents can offer a variety of skills and it is up to the teachers to match the parents and the curriculum subjects to the children's best interests. This can include maths, language, science...or whatever subject or topic needed covering.'

Evidence of improved continuity of parental involvement between nursery/primary/secondary transition was indicated by some link teachers. Parents stayed with one class teacher, helped in other areas in the school and often stayed at the primary school as they felt more confident and comfortable. Hearsay evidence also strongly indicates that once parents have become involved and supportive in the school, they are more involved in their children's education.

Shared Homework activities were set up in each project school. The project enabled some of the schools to 'have a clearer focus on shared homework activities'. An OFSTED report for one school stated:

> provision for developmental writing and reading are good. There is a popular and well-used library funded by City Challenge run by parents to provide books children take home to share with their parents.

Homework became 'integral and part of school life' while the main concern was 'Children and parental reliability in taking home and returning material' (link teacher).

Table 6.2 shows the shared homework activities in project schools in the third year.

Table 6.2 (Bawa, Annual Report 1996)

School	Shared homework in Literacy	Shared homework in Numeracy
N1	PACT	IMPACT
N2	Shared reading	Mathematical games
P1	Home–school reading record book	IMPACT
P2	FIR	IMPACT
P3	Home reading record sheet	IMPACT
P4	PACER	IMPACT
P5	PACT	IMPACT
P6	PACER/SPIR	IMPACT
P7	PACT	IMPACT
S1	Home–school diaries/information exchange by telephone for some community language speakers	

Key: PACT (Parents and Children and Teachers)
FIR (Family involvement in reading)
PACER (Parents and Children Enjoy Reading)
SPIR (School (P6) Parental Involvement with Reading)
IMPACT (Parental Involvement in Maths)

To meet Qualitative Targets 5 and 6 schools identified specific training for parents/governors/teachers. Parents were particularly interested in word processing and First Aid courses. At one school the word processing course enabled one parent to find paid work;

another to go on to further education and work experience, and one parent working part-time became employed full-time. Computers at the school were also used in the PACER classes. The parenting education courses proved to be very popular and parents were overwhelmingly positive about the courses. Training undertaken by parents helped to enhance their confidence and self-esteem, leading to increased support for children in and out of school, employment and/or further education for some parents. Table 6.3 gives examples of training taken up by parents in the second year.

Table 6.3 (Bawa, Annual Report 1995)

School	Training/other	Parents/Governors/ Teachers	Further Education/ Other
N1	PACT/PACER/ First Aid	Parents/Teachers	Support pupils
N2	Working with black parents; storytelling	Parents/Teachers	
P1	Bookmaking resources	Parents/Teachers	
P2	First Aid	Parents/Governors	
P3	INSET on Bullying	Welfare support	Playground support enhanced
P4	Setting up a bilingual books section in the library	Parents/Teachers	
P5	Setting up parents room/improving school grounds	Parents/Governors	
P6	Word processing	Parents	Further education; employment; support pupils
P7	Word processing/ First Aid	Parents/Governors	Further education; support pupils
S1	Makaton	Parents/Teachers	

Key spin-offs

Project Conference March 1994

The aim of this conference, held at the end of the first year, was to spread good practice and celebrate partnership in raising achievement in Newham schools.

Parents were specifically targeted both to attend and to take an active part in the seven workshops and presentations. Approximately 200 participants attended, including parents, teachers, officers, governors, parental education workers from the statutory and voluntary sector. The conference was opened by the Chair of Education Committee, stressing the importance of parental involvement and the needs of young people and the Chief Executive of City Challenge, pleased to be supporting a project with such commitment to parental involvement and raising achievement. Over 40 per cent of the participants were parents, being involved in the actual presentations and workshops as well as attending.

Schools found a definite increase in parental input afterwards, 'parents were buzzing with excitement and enthusiasm' (head teacher). The evaluation sheets confirmed the success of the conference:

'Brilliant meeting... a great opportunity to meet others aiming for the same goals.'

'Nice to see how successful parents groups can be.'

'Very happy to see that at last the idea of parental involvement as educators is supported. In 1960s many black parents did this with their children. I am one who did, but was discouraged from doing so.'

'It was good to see the teachers believing in parent involvement and in spirit.'

'The most interesting part was the involvement of parents with the presentation of ideas.'

(London Borough of Newham 1994)

Working in Partnership with Parents – An Action Guide for Schools
Working with the LEA strategy group consisting of representatives of schools, teachers, parents, governors, LEA workers and the voluntary sector, a key task was the development of a comprehensive, accessible set of guidelines. Consultation on content and format took place with all schools and a range of parent organisations and other agencies. A loose-leaf format was adopted to enable schools to use all or part of the guide as appropriate to them.

The Action Guide for Schools was published and launched at a conference in March 1995. This resource pack was intended to support schools in developing 'their own patterns of parental involvement and act as a check against which they can review their own practices' (Action Guide for Schools 1995). The Action Guide drew on good practice developed in City Challenge project schools, with contributions from other schools in the Borough. Case studies give all schools access to the lessons learnt and allow initiatives to be repeated or further developed in other schools. Each school in the Borough was given three copies and numerous copies have been sold locally and nationally.

As a follow on to the action guide, a leaflet 'Working in Partnership with Schools, a guide for parents' was published and distributed to parents of all schoolchildren in the Borough. The leaflet looks at ways of supporting children both in and out of school and has received positive feedback from numerous sources. The leaflet was later translated into different languages and published to cater for the growing refugee communities.

Two further leaflets published for parents were 'Helping your child with Reading, a guide for parents' and 'Helping your child with Mathematics, a guide for parents'. Both leaflets received a very positive response from parents and teachers.

Extension projects A and B

Project A – Parenting programmes

An extension to the main Action for Achievement project was made successfully in 1995. This would incorporate support and training in parenting skills for parents and carers (Samra 1999).

Successful programmes were held for each project school in English (mainly), Punjabi, Urdu, Somali and Bengali. Each course was evaluated and a focus group held six to eight weeks after completion. The feedback sheets were overwhelmingly positive about the value of the courses for parents. Their views include:

'I feel that I can manage my children better.'

'I have learned communication skills.'

'Reduce stress levels.'

'Being given a wider view of things.'

'I feel that I am generally more positive now to my children.'

A group of parents who had become involved in the school through the project and had just completed a parenting course, decided to participate in Theatre Venture – an East London Arts Company, to put on a production around parenting. This was very successful and the group of parents featured in the project conference in year four as well as in national seminars/conferences.

(Samra 1999).

Project B – Home visits for preschool children

Funding was made available to enable schools to make home visits for preschool children and leave resources, such as crayons, paper, scissors, for children to use at home. Schools generally endorsed the value of home visiting. The two nurseries saw this as invaluable and most schools planned to continue with the visits.

Working in Partnership with Parents Seminar 1997

This was an overwhelming success with over 150 delegates. The seminar was held to celebrate the European Year of Lifelong Learning and to launch Newham's Learning Community Strategy.

The panel included speakers from Education, Parents Support Network, Family Literacy, Early Years Unit, Social Services and Health Services, Councillors, Senior Education Officers and Titus Alexander (see Alexander 1997). The panel of speakers were followed by the workshops listed below with professionals and parents leading:

Action for Achievement Project
Early years
Parents Support Network
Family Literacy
Community Education and Youth Service – emphasising the aims and initiatives of the Learning Community Strategy
Managing Children
Health.

The seminar was concluded by presentations made by parents.

The evaluation gave very positive feedback and the City Challenge Action for Achievement project was highlighted as many initiatives would not have been possible without it.

(London Borough of Newham 1997)

Discussion of project outcomes

Raising pupil achievement was the main hoped-for outcome of the project and all the qualitative and quantitative targets were seen as important in meeting this goal. Each school had a different starting point and particular needs and therefore specific action plans were developed to meet project targets. It is important to remember the difficulty in establishing direct causal links between rises in levels of achievement and parental involvement.

The increase in parental involvement in fund-raising, curriculum and social events indicated parents being interested enough to venture into school – not an easy feat for some parents. Meeting other parents and teachers helped to 'break barriers' and led to parents becoming more aware and involved in the life of the school.

The evaluation surveyed parents and their children's views and stated that parents generally felt they had gained a great deal by being involved in school and how their views had changed as they became more aware. Verbatim comments from parents include:

'brilliant, it opened up the school to me'

'it's got me out and involved'

'I get to know what my child does'

'I love helping the children'

'teachers are easier to approach'

'it helps to know how to help my child'

'children more confident now'

'it helped with reading'

'home and school are very connected'

'can now speak to teachers, for example, if there is a problem'

'I wish I'd started earlier'

It must be impossible not to relate the experiences of these parents to their children and thus influence their children's attitudes and achievement. How can we not attribute parental involvement to pupil achievement – however little or extensive the achievement is in the long term?

The evaluation exercises show a snapshot of the events and attitudes of those involved. This in itself is important to validate the findings, indicate the progress made and help to give direction for future years. Evaluation can contribute to the overall picture and can help to identify some of the 'causes and effects' which are notoriously difficult to pin down definitely within a social/educational intervention such as City Challenge.

Class teachers were asked by the evaluator about the link between parental involvement and pupils' achievement. On the whole the responding class teachers subscribed to parental involvement as being a vehicle by which children's educational achievement might be enhanced.

Parents were asked, 'From doing "x" what do you feel you have learned about school and teachers?' Full and informative responses include:

'I respect them more; what they do and for all the hard work; very friendly school.'

'A lot of the teachers are not very cooperative; I have benefited; when I am in, D. (child) is relaxed; learned more how school runs, and about the teacher–pupil relationship; I am more relaxed and D is more open to teachers now.'

'I appreciate their [teachers] hard work, their patience, and their own time they put into it. They really care about the children. I always feel very welcomed.'

'They [teachers] are human, normal people. I used to be a pupil here, and more parents are involved now.'

'It's a thankless task, a hard job; teachers need someone (for example, parents) to help; they do really well, it's a good school.'

This is a linchpin question that goes to the heart of parental perceptions about, and understanding of, school. Responses indicate: a greater understanding of the purpose of school; acknowledged respect for teachers; appreciation of the challenges teachers face; qualities and skills that teachers possess...This was a core question too for the City Challenge initiative, hypothesised as it was on the premise that if parents gain greater understanding and knowledge of school and the educational process, then this has a positive effect on to their children's educational achievement. Such knowledge and understanding hopefully becomes cumulative over time, passing to future generations.

Children were also interviewed with their parents and asked about parental involvement. Overall there was strong affirmation regarding the maternal presence in school...provided positive endorsement for these children's mothers. Verbatim comments include:

'It helps with letters'

'With art in school, reading at home'

'Helps me to behave – I have to be good'

The pupils' views (from a sufficiently large numerical sample) were further expressed in their own handwriting. These represent one angle of the triangle and by and large, their views corroborate and affirm closer home–school links.

One way of involving parents was through the shared homework activities. Monitoring and evaluation reports indicated clearly that homework in Literacy and Numeracy appeared to be embedded and part of the school routine. In general the activities were perceived to be successful. Problems related to 'time, reliability of returns, having a watertight recording system'.

The majority of head teachers interviewed felt that children had achieved in Literacy and Numeracy as a direct consequence of their parents' involvement with the project. Predominantly, head teachers had 'a positive view that increased parental involvement has a number of spin-offs, not only related to children's (measurable) achievement'.

Improvement at Key Stage 1 and Key Stage 2 has been impossible to measure as SATs didn't take place certain years, the criteria changed, pupil mobility was quite high in some schools, and a fair number of children were from newly arrived refugee families who had not attended school previously.

Most schools saw the key element as curriculum/teaching activities to achieve this target rather than parental involvement. Some schools did see parental involvement as valuable support for teaching.

The monitoring and evaluation exercises provide accumulating and perhaps sufficient evidence to attest to the fact that involving parents in their children's education does serve to raise attainment. Apart from measurable gains in achievement, which the City Challenge Project has helped to show is possible, parental involvement can be conceptualised in terms of 'value-added' – that is, the parental ingredient is a welcome, additional factor, a bonus on top of all the educational ingredients that go to make up an efficient and effectively functioning school.

Regarding the effects of the project, one head teacher commented:

'City Challenge has given us a focus and impetus ... I can't understand how you can have an effective school without parental involvement.'

Current Learning Community initiatives

The Learning Community Strategy (LCS), launched in 1997, has parental involvement high on its agenda. Its activity drew upon the City Challenge experience, particularly as the coordinator was appointed Learning Community Project Director.

Although examination results are improving each year, there is still much that needs to be done. In a borough such as Newham, traditional attitudes to education among long-established communities and socio-economic factors conspire against the efforts of schools and the LEA to raise achievement (Learning Community Panel Meeting Report).

The LCS is to develop an education culture in all communities by increasing the popularity of education and the opportunities for learning outside schools and other traditional settings. The strategy also has a corporate dimension: all council departments and external partners contribute to specific projects. The Learning Community initiatives are monitored and evaluated (including external evaluation). The initiatives include:

Home–School Agreements – initially piloted in a number of EAZ schools, followed by INSET for all schools covering lessons learnt and good practice. Model home–school agreements for primary and secondary schools have resulted from the pilot work – consultation with parents will need to take place and amendments made as appropriate.

EAZ schools will have printed home–school agreements by September 1999. Feedback from parents where the agreements are already in place has been positive.

Homework Initiative. A great deal has been achieved in this area – the main focus being on launching successfully the homework initiative in all EAZ schools. EAZ schools were provided with funding for coordinating homework, INSET involved developing policies, procedures and an implementation plan. Schools developed homework policies from the Authority's draft policy framework, guidance for parents was published, schools were provided with commercial and LEA homework materials and practice tests for Key Stage 1 and Key Stage 2 as well as homework bags and basic homework equipment being provided for all pupils in nursery and primary schools.

Saturday schools aim to increase the motivation of, and participation by, children in the education and learning process by: improving the basic skills of children in Years 5 and 6; assisting them in the transition from primary to secondary school; access to a secondary school curriculum in Science, English, Maths, information technology and other subjects with teachers from primary and secondary schools.

Newham Summer School offers young people additional learning opportunities during August. This year's evaluation report, as in previous years, indicates a very successful third Summer School with over 2,500 places being provided for 8–16-year-olds (Summer School Reports 1998 and 1999). The programmes were available in all parts of the Borough, set up in partnership with the voluntary sector, local colleges, the council's leisure services and social services departments. The programmes offered a wide range of subjects and learning opportunities, which complement National Curriculum priorities as well as specific provision in basic skills.

Study support for pupils in Years 10 and 11 offer support for out-of-school-hours learning for all secondary schools. All schools reported on the successful impact of study support on GCSE results.

Other Learning Community initiatives include, **Parental Involvement** initiatives; **Accelerated learning** initiative and **GCSE Community Language Provision**.

Based on the City Challenge Project, a **Raising Achievement – Parental Involvement Project** has been funded through the Single Regeneration Budget, for nine primary schools and a designated post in the Green Street area of the Borough. **Family Learning projects – Family Literacy, Family Numeracy** and **It's a Man Thing** (fathers and reading) are running in a number of schools during 1999 to 2000. These projects are supported by external funding through the Standards Fund and the fathers and reading project in partnership with the Community Education and Development Centre (CEDC) – see Chapter 9.

Raising achievement continues to be a top priority in Newham and projects such as the City Challenge Action for Achievement enabled schools to:

do what we always wanted but never had the space or time to do so.

(link teacher)

In an area such as Newham, we need to continue to support parents in supporting their children and working in partnership to raise educational achievement.

References

(For London Borough of Newham, contact Bala Bawa, Beckton Globe, 1 Kingsford Way, London E6 5JQ)

Action Guide for Schools (1995) *Working in Partnership with Parents* London: London Borough of Newham.
Alexander, T. (1997) *Empowering Parents: Families as the foundation of a learning society.* London: National Children's Bureau.
Bawa, B. (1994–1997) *City Challenge Action for Achievement Monitoring Reports.* London: London Borough of Newham.
Hegarty, S. (1989) *Boosting Educational Achievement – Report of the Independent Inquiry into Educational Achievement in the London Borough of Newham* (The Hegarty Report). Education Department.
London Borough of Newham (1994) *Parental Involvement Conference Report.*
London Borough of Newham (1997) *Working in Partnership with Parents, Seminar Report.*
London Borough of Newham (1998 and 1999) *Summer School Reports.*

London Borough of Newham (1999a) *Learning Community Panel Meeting Report.*

London Borough of Newham (1999b) *Learning Community Progress Report.*

London Borough of Newham (1999c) *Newham Education Action Zone, Action Plan 1999 to 2000.*

Samra, B. (1999) 'Supporting parents through parenting programmes', in Wolfendale, S. and Einzig, H. (eds) *Parenting Education and Support, New Opportunities*, Chapter 8. London: David Fulton Publishers.

Wolfendale, S. (1994–98) *City Challenge Action for Achievement Evaluation Reports.* Psychology Department, University of East London, Stratford Campus, Romford Road, London E15 4LZ.

Wolfendale, S. (1996) 'The contribution of parents to children's achievement in school: policy and practice in the London Borough of Newham', in Bastiani, J. and Wolfendale, S. (eds) *Home–School Work in Britain, Review, Reflection and Development.* London: David Fulton Publishers.

Chapter 7

Parents and the school working together to achieve success: one school's experience

Angus Hardie and Margaret Alcorn

In determining the factors by which active parental involvement can impact positively on school effectiveness, we will focus on the experience of one school in an area of multiple deprivation. We will describe the evolution of the INSTEP Project within the school and the strategies that were developed to support effective home–school working. We will try to assess the impact of INSTEP on the effectiveness of the school. Finally we will describe in outline the New Community High School initiative in Scotland, and how it will articulate with current provision.

The context

Castlebrae Community High School is situated in the south east of Edinburgh and serves one of the most socially and economically deprived communities in the east of Scotland. In 1991 adult unemployment was more than twice the Edinburgh average and the community was characterised by poor health, low self-esteem and an overwhelming sense of hopelessness. Vandalism and crime were rife, and housing in the area was basic and badly maintained. It was an area that no-one wanted to live in; local people with drive and ambition moved out at the first opportunity.

The impact of these factors in the school was significant. Staff worked hard to create a caring and supportive environment, but this meant that pupils were not always offered sufficient challenge to succeed in academic terms. Levels of attainment in Scottish Certificate of Education national examinations were among the worst in Scotland and the roll had fallen steadily from 900 to less than 300. Parents who valued education usually chose to send their child to a school out of the area. Many local people who had been educated in Castlebrae remembered a negative experience which further tainted their perceptions of the school. By any measure, the school had lost the confidence and respect of the local community.

At this time the local Education Authority took the decision to close the school, and a new management team was appointed in the school on a temporary basis to manage the closure. However the options for closure offered to the community were not considered acceptable and the decision was eventually reversed. The new management team now had the remit of producing and implementing a plan which would reverse the decline of the school.

From the start it was clear that the school needed to make significant changes to all aspects of its work and that these changes had to be responsive to the special needs of the community. For example the curriculum was congruent with national guidelines and advice, but it was clearly not delivering education of an appropriate standard to local children. The teachers were dedicated and hard-working, but exam results and destination analyses demonstrated that the current methodologies and classroom relationships were not leading to success. There was something of a beleaguered feel within the school; a sense of running very fast only to stand still. The teachers and the pupils were characterised by an almost fatalistic sense of powerlessness.

Before embarking on any development work, it was essential that attention was paid to the need to change the culture of the school. Management had to 'change the belief' so that they could 'change the performance'. For example, in common with many colleagues, teachers in the school were of the opinion that development planning, target-setting, and the measurement of performance belonged in the world of business, and had little relevance for education. The management team made clear that if the school were to improve, then ways to measure progress had to be found. This was not a simple matter. At that time there was no local or national support for target-setting, and no indicators existed which could be used to measure the success of the school. No framework for school development planning was available, and school staff had to give careful consideration to designing appropriate tools for gauging progress. It is interesting, and no doubt gratifying to school staff, that each of these issues have now been addressed nationally, and all schools throughout Scotland are expected to take account of them. The publication of 'How good is our school?' in September 1996, 'Raising Standards – Setting Targets' in August 1998 and 'Standards and Quality in Scottish Schools 1995–1998' in the spring of 1999 has ensured that development planning, performance indicators and negotiated targets are concerns in every Scottish school.

A significant discussion centred on the need to ensure that the measurements chosen were indeed indicative of real success, and not just a reflection of what was easily measured. Exam results and attendance rates had to be read in the context of the school's circumstances if they were to have meaning. The outcomes of the planning exercise in Castlebrae became the 'success criteria' for the school. Eight criteria for success were agreed, and targets for one year and five years were set against each of these criteria. The criteria were:

- more students;
- better examination results;
- more students directly entering employment/higher education/ further education;
- improved attendance and punctuality;
- improved behaviour and attitudes;
- more parental and community involvement;
- increased staff and student morale;
- better image of the school.

In order to deliver on the targets (described by the chair of the local authority education committee as 'ambitious') priorities were established and working groups set up to plan the way ahead. Staff were encouraged to think creatively and innovatively. The prevailing sense was of moving in uncharted territory where the old rules no longer applied. For example at this time the division between education and business was clearly defined. As a first step in the journey of improvement, the school set out to build partnerships with industry and business to a degree which was very unusual. With this advice and support, new pre-vocational courses were introduced into the third and fourth year curriculum to prepare students for employment. A Business Advisory Group was set up to act as consultants for the changes to the school's personal and social development programme. A planned and progressive programme of education-industry links was established.

Other significant changes were made. Anti-bullying policies were developed and implemented, and a newly developed teaching and learning policy became the linchpin of all the change within the school. At each stage the parent members of the School Board were consulted and their support sought. Although none of these initiatives was in itself new, the scale of development, the methodology adopted and the number of fronts on which action was taken combined to give a sense of genuine innovation.

Underpinning and supporting all the developments was a complete reassessment of the relationship the school had with its parents and specifically attempts were made to address the largely negative perceptions of local people, particularly those with school-aged children. Staff had to devise strategies that would start to rebuild lost confidence in the ability of the school to deliver excellence. Friends in the business community suggested surveying parents in an attempt to define what they considered to be the characteristics of an effective school and to assess their view of Castlebrae's performance against those characteristics. To do this, a list incorporating a wide range of features describing an effective secondary school was drawn up. A series of home visits were arranged to survey parents on which features they considered to be most important when choosing a secondary school. They were then asked to score Castlebrae against each of these features. Where there was a significant discrepancy between those two ratings, this indicated to the school an area that required improvement.

The results held no surprises; parents wanted effective learning, more and better jobs and a safe environment for their children, and it was clear from the early surveys that they did not consider the school able to deliver in these areas. The information thus gathered was used to ensure that plans for developing the school took full account of parental perceptions. This innovative methodology proved so useful in giving the school a clear indication of priorities for development that it has now become a biennial event.

Other measurements for success were also developed. For example, in common with colleagues in many schools, staff were concerned about student behaviour and were keen to implement various strategies to support improvement in this area. Discussions on how progress in this could be effectively measured were long and hard. As with many measurements, the most obvious answer was not always the best. Rates of referral to management and exclusion were discounted as being simplistic and not genuinely reflective of progress. Eventually we agreed to test staff and student perceptions of behaviour and use these as the indicator of success (parents' views were sought through the survey). By this measure, progress has been consistent in the intervening years.

Additionally the school began to survey staff and student morale on a regular basis, using questionnaires developed for this purpose. This exercise allowed managers within the school to monitor progress with some of the less easily measurable success criteria such as 'increased staff and student morale' and 'improved behaviour and attitudes'. Over a five-year period, the results proved fascinating and the indications were of steady progress in most areas. More students said that they were happier in school, that good behaviour was rewarded and that their chances of success in exams had improved. Fewer staff felt stressed, and increasingly few expressed a wish that they worked in another school. From the perspective of parents perhaps the most significant change was in the number of students who felt they were experiencing success. Staff felt reassured that this offered clear evidence that policies on the use of praise, behaviour support, etc., were being successfully implemented and that slow but steady progress was being made.

Despite all these positive indicators, in 1992 staff became frustrated by the slow pace of change and by their continued inability to impact on the low value that many local parents gave to the education of their children. It was clear that this was continuing to have a seriously damaging effect on pupil motivation. The reality was that the problems of the Craigmillar community were many and complex and that the school, working in isolation, had a very limited ability to make a meaningful impact. The management team, with the support of local politicians, decided to apply for urban aid funding to set up a new resource in the school with the aims of creating a step-change in the development of home–school relations and of devising new approaches to the challenge of how to maximise the positive influence of the home environment on a young person's education. The critical difference between this initiative and the vast amount of work that takes place elsewhere in the field of home–school relations is that the exclusive focus for the project was to be a secondary school. This initiative became the INSTEP Project.

The INSTEP Project

For a school to establish a project which had at its core a remit to work with parents, is a powerful statement to all stakeholders – staff, students, other agencies and parents. In the case of INSTEP the force of this statement was emphasised by the size of the project – four project workers, admin support and a coordinator. An early decision was that the coordinator should sit within the senior management team of the school, ensuring strong links and a coherent approach. The establishment of INSTEP blew the dust off much of the rhetoric about the role of parents in schools and placed a more forceful set of expectations on all concerned to live up to what had in many cases been unfulfilled promises.

Funding for the project was sought at a time of great change in the school. There was a mood within the school staff of 'backs to the wall' and a real sense of common purpose and commitment to succeed in turning the school around. However, in terms of the detail of the project's remit and structure there had been little consultation with any of the key stakeholders both within the school and with the other agencies who contributed to the life of the school. Therefore when the funding came through and staff began to be appointed, it became apparent that one of the first tasks was to diffuse a high level of scepticism and suspicion as to the project's intentions, and then to negotiate a variety of appropriate working relationships both within the school and in the wider community.

From the start it was clear that there was little within the project's stated aims and objectives which could not in some way be construed as infringing on someone else's area of responsibility or to some extent implying a criticism of past performance. For instance, elements of the liaison with parents and home seemed to impact on the pastoral role of guidance; local social workers took a keen interest in the team's presence and tried to offload some of their non-statutory responsibilities; the careers service became very protective of their responsibilities to support school-leavers in the transition into work; education welfare service workers were openly hostile towards what they perceived as the creaming off of their preferred role of supporting parents while leaving them with the traditional and unpopular function of 'truant officer'.

The project was faced with something of a paradox. The school, at senior management level, recognised that it needed to take a quantum leap in many areas of its performance. In order to effect these changes the school required a device to 'hold the door open' long enough for the new mindsets and practices to become the norm. Staff had to be given time to see that the perceived threat behind these changes was less than at first thought. In many respects the INSTEP Project represented this 'door jamming' device and therefore, while it was a priority to foster good relations with everyone at the outset, it was equally important to be aware that the project had the subtext of facilitating change at all levels as part of its remit.

In an environment where there are several agencies operating alongside one another, it is generally recognised that the different professional boundaries and cultures can result in less than ideal collaboration. Both teachers and staff from other agencies inevitably operate within their own comfort zones on a day to day basis. If the ambition to achieve a step-change in the overall level of performance of the school was to be met, some means of stretching these comfort zones had to be found. The implication for the project, if INSTEP was to be the catalyst for this change, was that it had to occupy the uncomfortable space at the edge of these comfort zones. It would propose changes and absorb the reactions, sometimes hostile, until the adjustments had become embedded in the working practices of those involved.

The location of this non-teaching project within the school with a remit to impact on levels of pupil attainment inevitably created certain tensions. Indeed the head-teacher has subsequently confessed to a private aspiration for the project that it would do just that in order to challenge assumptions and ingrained work practices. The key challenge for the project was to manage these tensions creatively, to ensure that they remained healthy and were able to provide the catalyst for practices and attitudes within the school to change. An example of the way in which INSTEP staff approached this can be seen in the evolving relationship they enjoyed with the Guidance team in the school. Initial suspicion of the new project was in danger of becoming outright hostility when two members of the team were located in the Guidance office. There was a danger that roles would become unclear and that new working practices might be seen to imply criticism of the old. Regular joint meetings, sustained clear focus, a sensitive understanding of boundaries and other issues were all required. Both sides learned important lessons from this joint working and the school – and the project – emerged richer and stronger from the experience.

It was recognised from the outset that the project would have to be highly flexible in terms of the approaches which were used in order to develop more effective home–school relations. There were many parents who felt either intimidated or excluded from the school and would require high levels of support and advocacy in order to re-engage to any meaningful extent with the school. By the same token the school had developed some attitudes and practices towards parents which had become deeply embedded over a long period of time and it was clear that these would need to be challenged if any real and lasting change was to take place.

In order to achieve any meaningful progress in relation to changing parental attitudes or school practices it was necessary to adopt a somewhat chameleon approach. If the project had presented itself to school staff as being a resource which was exclusively for parents, the opportunities to work closely with teachers and school systems would have been much fewer. Consequently the project team evolved a pattern of work that shifted over time and circumstance – at certain times of the year the project worked hand in glove with the school and at others the distance from the school was greater, and much closer to the parents. For instance at the time of the year when S2 students make their subject choices for Standard Grade, the school required a great deal of liaison with parents. To this end the project made great efforts to support this process by taking information out to parents and bringing parents in to speak with school staff. At other times of the year, such as just prior to the start of each new school session, when concern amongst parents of new first year students could be high, project staff spent a great deal of time working very closely with parents, allaying any fears they had or giving information of all types as and when it was needed.

In those first years, with short-term funding, the pressure was on to establish some early indications of success. This was driven not only by the need to lay down the foundations for the case for further funding but also to establish a degree of credibility with the most immediate set of interested observers – the teachers. The feature which most teachers identified with the project was the work to increase parental involvement in the school. The most commonly recognised indicator of parental interest as far as school staff are concerned tends to be levels of attendance at parents' evenings. Although not necessarily the most imaginative or meaningful measure of parental interest, the project could not ignore the importance the teaching staff attached to parents evenings. Consequently in the early stages of the project, this area became a major focus of attention for the project. Traditionally attendance figures in the school were very low – no higher than 20–25 per cent. With intensive home-visiting these figures were brought up to an average of 75 per cent. The project also took on the task of revamping the way the school went about organising these events. Everything was changed, from the timing and type of invitation that went out to parents, to the location in the school where teachers were to meet with parents. Significant changes were made to the reception that parents received on arrival and the sort of information they were given to help them find their way round the school. Although during surveys, parents expressed increased levels of satisfaction with the revised format of these evenings, the impression conveyed was that it was more a case of these events being less of an ordeal than previously experienced, rather than being viewed as a positive opportunity to obtain useful information from their children's teachers.

Allied to this emphasis on parents' evenings, the project's other initial priority was to establish a broad base of relationships with parents. Again driven partly by the perceived lack of time due to the nature of the funding, project staff made several blanket visits across all year groups using any opportunity which presented itself on which to hang the visit. In the early stages of this programme of home-visiting, as project staff were introducing themselves to parents as a resource to be called upon, the objective was simply to establish a basis for a future working relationship without being particularly specific about what form that support should take. This strategy proved to be a double-edged sword. On the one hand the project team was successful in establishing a wide number of very strong relationships with a significant number of the school's parents. On the other hand, as a result of the project team not being specific enough about what they would be able to offer parents, the greatest demands came from parents who were more familiar with the idea of external agencies becoming involved in the life of the family. Typically these families were likely to be experiencing a range of other problems. Very often they were actively engaged with a number of other agencies such as social work, and as a result of their circumstances had very great difficulty in creating the space within the home agenda for education and the school.

In danger of losing all focus and becoming drawn into areas of work for which the staff were neither qualified nor funded to carry out, the project became much more circumspect as to the criteria for justifying working with any particular family. Beyond the point of transition from primary to secondary school when all parents are visited, the onus was on parents to demonstrate a degree of receptiveness to becoming involved with the project. Consequently the nature of the project's work with parents has evolved into a programme which is much more targeted, with a focus either on specific groups of parents or on particular events during the year.

Six years on, the project is now well established in the area both with local residents and local schools. During that time the team has had a relatively free hand to explore different approaches and methods of improving the home–school relationship with particular reference to its impact on pupil performance.

One of the main conclusions at this stage is that given the context for the project, working with parents as the sole strategy could never achieve the sort of results which were being looked for at the outset. Partly because the main focus for the project was the secondary school and partly because of the severe levels of social and economic hardship present in the area, the impact of working with parents when seen in isolation from other strategies is always going to be limited. However when used to underscore other initiatives – be that developing a programme of out-of-school learning or offering a resource to support school leavers as they move into the world of work – the value of this work becomes much more evident.

Reflecting on the six years of the project, there is now a sense of having fully explored the parameters of what is possible and/or appropriate in the immediate context. While the aims remain the same in terms of trying to encourage more active and effective parental involvement, the approaches have evolved considerably over that time. To a large extent the emphasis has shifted away from trying to encourage more involvement of parents in the school itself to one which encourages more active interest in their children's education from the perspective of the home environment. The challenge of giving parents the confidence to believe that they can play a vital role in shaping the outcome of their children's education is most likely to be successful if that work takes place in the home. Consequently this has placed a much greater premium on the quality of information which parents receive and on making sure that parents are able to understand and respond appropriately. This approach still requires a strong relationship between the home and the school to be maintained. Traditionally schools have not made it a priority to monitor the nature, quality and timing of the information it sends to parents. Often the only contact is at times of difficulty, and at set piece parents' consultation meetings. Frequently all communications are in writing, and may be couched in language that parents find difficult to comprehend. INSTEP has piloted a more proactive approach towards monitoring home–school interactions. Computer software has been adapted to permit all contact between home and school to be logged and identified as being either of a positive or negative nature. This technology presents an opportunity to create an overview of all previous contact with a parent and to establish whether this profile has enough balance of positive elements to engender a healthy and positive home–school relationship.

Impact of INSTEP

The impact of the project on the effectiveness of the school is not easily measured in discrete terms. Because it was set up at a time of significant development within the school, its contribution has become entwined with many other initiatives designed to advance the school. What is certain is that as an important strand in this progression, it has supported and enhanced the experience of children and their parents within the Craigmillar community. Today the school has begun to enjoy significant success. In 1997 it was the winner of the first Scottish Schools Ethos Award. In 1998 the Scottish Consultative Council on the Curriculum selected the school as the subject of their publication 'A School With A Sense Of Purpose', which recommended the Learning and Teaching Policy within the school and the methodology used to develop and implement this as an example of excellent practice. In 1999 the school achieved Investors in People status, the first local school to do so. A local authority review of the school in January 1999 reported that:

> parents are satisfied that standards of behaviour are good. Almost all those interviewed expressed confidence in the school and felt that its reputation and standing in the community has improved greatly in recent years.

The returns from the biennial survey of parental and anecdotal evidence from within the community suggest the school is now viewed very differently by local people, and by other important constituencies such as colleagues within the teaching profession and local politicians, particularly those who were in favour of the original decision to close the school. The percentage of local people who are now choosing to send their children to Castlebrae has steadily increased and many others now see the school as an acceptable second choice. This represents a complete turnaround in the circumstances which faced the school six or seven years ago. The impact of the work of the project on local children is harder to assess, as they tend to respond only to their own experience and have no concept of the changes within the school over the years. However several of the young people who have entered university of college in recent years are clear that INSTEP was a significant factor in supporting their success.

A more indirect measure of the success that Castlebrae has enjoyed can be detected in the adoption at national level of many of the strategies that were so new to education in these early days. In recent months, the new Scottish Executive has published a draft Bill 'Improving our Schools – Consultation on the Improvement in Scottish Education Bill', which includes reference to school planning, target-setting and the use of performance indicators – all major elements in the success that Castlebrae has enjoyed. The strategic focus in this consultation document on 'Raising Standards' is one that sits comfortably with the developments put in place within the school.

Although it is difficult to separate the role of INSTEP now from other elements within the school it is widely acknowledged as having played a key role. While it is difficult to draw a precise correlation between improved school effectiveness and any specific strategy, it is widely accepted that the quality of the home school relationship has improved significantly. There is also now a consensus that the project has been instrumental in taking forward the home school agenda within the school's frame of reference and that this has contributed very positively towards the school's improving performance. As an indication of the progress which has been achieved over the period of Instep's existence two measures of the school's performance are set below.

Standard Grade Examination Performance

	1994	1999
3 or more awards (Grades 1–6)	56%	92%
3 or more awards (Grades 1–4)	31%	53%
3 or more awards (Grades 1–2)	7%	11%

School leaver destination analysis

	1993	1999
Unemployed	24%	5%
Employed	15%	60%
Moving into full-time FE/HE	2%	8%

Partly due to these statistics, the project has attracted widespread interest and in particular from politicians as senior as Frank Field, who visited the project as Minister for Social Security. Perhaps the most significant seal of approval on the work of the INSTEP team came in April 1999 when the project was mainstreamed and became part of the structure of the school. This was a significant moment in the life of the project, and indicated the confidence the local authority had in the work of the team and the results they had produced. It placed the project firmly within the Education Department's strategic plans for the area. After six years of short-term funding, it took away the insecurity of constantly seeking re-funding, and allowed INSTEP staff to focus more directly on the needs of local youngsters.

New Community Schools

This mainstreaming of INSTEP was a recognition that a school's effectiveness could be significantly enhanced by the presence of this sort of resource. However in a climate when schools are coming under ever greater pressure to achieve better and better results, attention is now turning to a new agenda in the hope that this might lead to some sort of solution or way forward for the future. This new agenda also happens to place a key role for parents at its centre but within a broader context than has been the case up until now. In Scotland the development of New Community Schools is at the heart of the government's strategy to promote social inclusion and to raise educational standards. In its prospectus inviting bids for pilot project funding, the Government stated that these schools 'will embody the fundamental principle that the potential of all children can be realised only by addressing their needs in the round – and that this requires an integrated approach by all those involved'.

Douglas Osler, HM Senior Inspector of Schools, described the philosophy that lies behind the initiative as focusing on 'the learning child rather than the school...about all of the children's needs and circumstances, about learning and growing'. As such this commitment accurately reflects the experience of INSTEP and Castlebrae. Integration of service provision – education, social work, adult and community education, health care and health promotion are the main services proposed – is expected to unlock the potential of schools to break into the repeating patterns of failure and underachievement that beset so many children living in disadvantaged communities (see Chapters 1 and 3). And although the government has stopped short of prescribing a model which the New Community Schools should follow, a number of essential requirements have been identified – one of which refers to importance of engaging with families in order to empower them to raise their expectations of their children and themselves.

Douglas Osler describes the aim as being 'education plus'. In Castlebrae, which has been identified as one of the first pilot projects, the intention is that it will take the form of 'INSTEP plus' as so many of the ingredients of this new proposal can be seen as being a natural extension to the progress that has already occurred. The crucial difference is that this proposal begins to take proper account of all the other factors which influence a child's progress in school and recognises the need to design and deliver a service provision which reflects this much more holistic view of a child's learning.

This first phase of these pilot projects is designed to encourage the development of as wide a range of different models of New Community School as possible. In many cases the co-location of services on one campus is being pursued as the predominant feature. In others, including the Craigmillar project, a cluster approach will be adopted. In the Craigmillar context, this will focus on shifting interagency practices throughout the area and the development of a more strategic approach to cross-sectorial working. A family support service is to be established by reconfiguring a number of existing resources. This new service will link with families from the earliest opportunity – through antenatal clinics and postnatal check ups – and aims to maintain a consistency of involvement thereafter, with an appropriate shifting focus to take account of the age and stage of the young person and the composition of the family. The emphasis and priority for the new resources is to be directed towards the early years although the contact with the home and the key role that is being spelt out for parents is expected to continue throughout secondary school.

However there are some good reasons to be cautious when it comes to setting out the expectations of what this experiment can deliver. The New Community School concept is based on the model of the Full Service School which has been developed in the United States (again, see Chapters 1 and 3). Evaluation of the Full Service School points to an increased take-up of services but it is less clear whether the initiative has made such a marked impact on educational attainment. Also, interagency working is not new. If full integration of services is to represent a significant step forward and achieve the sort of breakthrough in service delivery which is being spoken about, the lessons of the past must be taken into account. Rightly the government states that a new management structure and interdisciplinary team working will be needed and are putting in extra money to facilitate this. However the government has left it to the schools to find the solution to arguably the greatest barrier to success: ensuring professional agreement and effective interdisciplinary work. This has proved difficult in the past and where it has been achieved it has required a great deal of effort around coordination, building trust and the development of appropriate training opportunities. Agencies that have fared very differently in recent years in terms of budget cuts are unlikely to come to the table with the same appetite for change. A period of intensive planning involving young people, school and other staff, community agencies and businesses is associated with the more successful Full Service Schools. According to the coordinator of one multiagency centre in California: 'It is difficult to overestimate the amount of time collaboration takes.'*

The New Community School strategy is in its infancy and already there are concerns as to whether it will be adequately funded and given enough time by the government to make the sort of impact being sought. However in the context of Craigmillar there are grounds for optimism. The experience of the INSTEP Project in terms of creating a climate for change and facilitating effective interagency work, presents as a model which, with some modification, could be transferred into many of the communities which are piloting new approaches.

---

* *Children, Families and Learning – a new agenda for learning.* Scottish Council Foundation.

PART 3

Chapter 8

Starting early with books

Barrie Wade and Maggie Moore

Introduction

The focus of this chapter is on literacy development and early experiences at school. We argue that home interactions with parents and carers are crucial for later educational development and that book sharing plays a central role in laying the foundations of literacy. The pilot Bookstart project in Birmingham in 1992 made gifts of books to families of 6–9-month-old babies via health clinics and health visitors.

Initial analysis of that pilot study provided encouraging results (Wade and Moore 1993); so did an intensive follow-up study of home activities and book behaviour when the children were 2½ to 3 years of age (Wade and Moore 1996a, b). In this chapter we present evidence from a further follow-up of the original Bookstart children at five years of age, when they had entered and settled into their primary schools. First, we review evidence for parental interaction and specifically book-oriented behaviour with young children at home. Then we briefly describe the Bookstart project and its findings. Next we describe the organisation of our school-age follow-up and present its results. Finally, we discuss the implications of the findings for literacy and learning and for further research.

Early parental involvement in learning

If parents involve themselves actively in their children's development and learning, then evidence shows that children achieve more. Jean Piaget (for example 1952, 1954) firmly established that young children learn through interaction with people and objects in their environment. Far from being passive observers, infants learn through exploring and through action. Adults are essential in providing both encouragement and opportunities to engage with a variety of experiences. They also provide models of behaviour. Bronfenbrenner (for example 1979) stresses that development is best effected if adult–child relationships are warm and non-dominating. In other words, following Piaget, a c̣ needs guidance, but the opportunity to discover and practise is aṇ essential, so that control of objects and situations is gradually learned. Bronfenbrenner argues that the best kind of interaction is reciprocal, with adult and child taking turns and sharing roles. The safe presence of a well-known adult is a prerequisite for the risk taking that leads to learning. Ainsworth and Bell (1970) showed that one-year-olds in three different contexts (alone; with a stranger; with a parent) explored a playroom more in the company of parents. We know too that young babies exhibit learning potential through responsiveness, discrimination, imitation and reciprocal behaviour (Richards 1974, Bower 1979). Appleton *et al.* (1975) demonstrated that by four or five months of age a child responds differently to voices; for example, will smile when mother speaks. Just as early experimentation with sounds at about three months gives pleasure to both child and parent, so the reciprocal pleasures of book sharing, rhyme and story are motivating and pleasure giving from, say, nine months onwards.

Early book sharing

There is plenty of evidence (for example Bryant and Bradley 1985, Brice Heath 1989, Hannon and James 1990) that the active involvement of parents through rhymes, stories and books lays the foundations of literacy in children's early years. In particular, the child's early experiences of story and making stories (Wade 1984) and sharing books (Wells 1985, Toomey 1993) affect educational progress. Wells (1986), Butler (1988) and Juel (1988) all argue the importance of a head start at the onset of schooling; those children who have established literacy foundations by school age are likely to achieve more in their school years. Bus *et al.* (1995) put the matter succinctly:

> pre schoolers who are already ahead at the start of formal reading instruction tend to maintain their position relative to other children at school during the stage of formal reading instruction. (p. 5)

Their review of existing research on adult-child book sharing in the preschool years showed a quantitative relationship to growth of language, emergent literacy and achievement in reading. Scarborough and Dobrich (1994) corroborate this relationship between reading achievement and early book sharing. Thus there is plenty of evidence to support the conclusion of Debaryshe (1993) that it may be important to introduce books to pre schoolers at a very early age. The Bookstart pilot study commenced in Birmingham in 1992 and set out to influence book sharing and develop positive attitudes to books in a group of families with young babies living in the inner city.

Bookstart: the beginnings

The national pilot of Bookstart provided a free pack for a cohort of 300 families who had babies approximately nine months old. As well as a children's book, the pack contained a bookmark, poster and poem card, together with information about library facilities, the value of book sharing and book purchase. Investigations by questionnaire showed that families valued the pack. It led to positive attitudes to books, more library enrolments, more book sharing with babies, more book club membership and more book purchase (Wade and Moore 1993).

Some two years after the pilot an intensive, qualitative, controlled study was conducted involving a random sample of 29 of the original families. Structured interviews revealed that the Bookstart group gave higher priority to looking at books and were more likely to give books as presents than did a comparison group. They also visited libraries more often and engaged more often in book sharing with their child (Wade and Moore 1996a). Observations of parent–child book sharing within the home revealed that Bookstart children showed more interest in and concentration on the book and were more active in pointing to the text and pictures and trying to turn pages than the comparison group who had not received the Bookstart pack. Their verbal behaviour also showed they participated substantially more actively than comparison group members; they made more predictions and joined in more with the adult's reading; they also asked and answered substantially more questions (Wade and Moore 1996b). These positive behaviours we concluded were likely to be the result of regular and repeated experience of book sharing stimulated by the Bookstart pack. These findings also stimulated our interest to discover whether effects were even more long-lasting, that is to school age. Accordingly, we planned a further stage in our longitudinal study.

School-age achievement of Bookstart children

Procedure

By 1997 Bookstart babies from the Birmingham pilot, described above, had reached school age, so it became possible to discover what kind of baseline in literacy the Bookstart youngsters brought with them to school. Accordingly, a sample of children was randomly selected from the families who had provided the evidence referred to above. One of the problems with follow-up research is that families move, sometimes several times. Despite this difficulty of tracing subjects, a group of 41, satisfactory for intensive research and comparison, was obtained. All parents gave permission for their children's primary schools to be contacted.

With the cooperation of Birmingham Local Education Authority and head teachers, access was obtained to the city's Baseline Assessment procedures and specifically to the Baseline results for our sample. The Birmingham Baseline Assessment (Birmingham City Council 1996) had been made jointly by staff involved in the children's reception classrooms and focused on achievements both in English and mathematics through careful observation of children's behaviour. Briefly, there are three assessments made in English: speaking and listening; reading; writing. There are three others in mathematics: using and applying mathematics; number (focus on counting); shape, space and measures (focus on shape). In each of these six assessment areas the child's achievement is assessed on a four-point scale for which clear criteria are laid down. Thus, for example, in reading a child scores 0 if there is no observable evidence of developing an interest in books and print. If the child is assessed as developing this interest she/he scores 1. If the child can recognise familiar individual words in responding to books and print the score is 2. If the child can read to an adult simple personal or published books of their own choice a score of 3 is given. The Baseline Assessment procedures, therefore, give a professional observation of children's achievements in six important areas and are completed when the child has settled down into his/her new class. A great advantage of the Birmingham Baseline is that for each child it provides five aspects of background evidence:

- gender
- home language
- ethnic group
- nursery experience
- date of birth.

We used these criteria to rigorously select a comparison group child from the same class. This procedure avoided possible bias on the part of researchers or class teachers and gave us a matched group of 41 children to compare with the Bookstart group.

Results

Speaking and listening provided similar numbers of children (about 20 per cent) achieving a maximum score of 3. However, almost twice as many in the Bookstart group scored 2 as in the comparison group and the only scores of 0 were all in the comparison group. Thus, as Figure 8.1 shows, the Bookstart group produced better results for Speaking and Listening. The difference in the range of scores is shown in standard deviations (Bookstart 0.7675; comparison 0.9253). While the Bookstart mean score of 1.7561 is higher than the comparison group, the difference is not statistically significant.

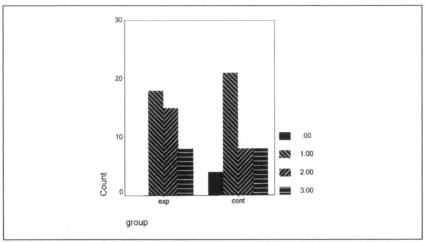

Figure 8.1 Speaking and listening

Similarly, for reading there were no scores of 0 in the Bookstart group, though about 17 per cent of the comparison group scored nil. About 10 per cent of the comparison group, but nearly twice as many in the Bookstart group, scored 2. Again, the only maximum scores of 3 (about 15 per cent) were all in the Bookstart group. Thus, as Figure 8.2 shows, Bookstart children were, as a whole, ahead of the comparison group in reading. The Bookstart group mean is 1.4634 (SD 0.7449), compared with 0.9268 (SD 0.5191), and this difference is very highly significant (t = 3.784, p = < 0.001).

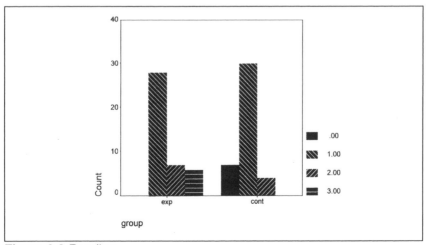

Figure 8.2 Reading

In writing there was no difference in numbers of lower performing children with the same number (about 7 per cent) scoring 0. However, twice as many Bookstart children scored 2 than in the comparison group and, again, the only two maximum scores were in the Bookstart group. Figure 8.3 records this superiority of Bookstart children at the higher levels of writing performance. Although the Bookstart group mean is higher (1.3171, SD = 0.6870, compared with 1.0976, SD = 0.4901) the difference is not statistically significant.

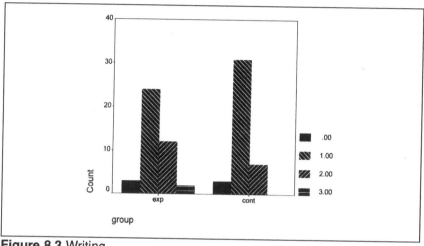

Figure 8.3 Writing

For using and applying mathematics there are smaller differences, but as Figure 8.4 shows, these are in favour of the Bookstart children who, as a group, achieve higher scores than the comparison group. The Bookstart group mean of 1.4878 (SD = 0.8978) compares with 1.2683 (SD = 0.8667), but the difference is not statistically significant.

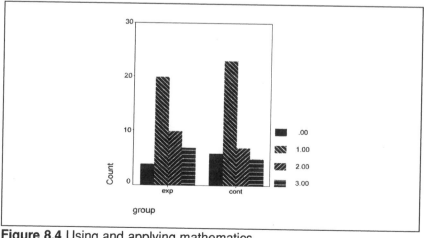

Figure 8.4 Using and applying mathematics

In number there are clearer advantages for the Bookstart children, who score more 2s and are the only group to record 3. Also, as Figure 8.5 shows, the comparison group scores more 0s in number assessment. The mean for the Bookstart group is 1.5122 (SD = 0.6753), compared with 1.0976 (SD = 0.6247), and this is a highly significant difference (t = 2.886, p = < 0.01).

In shape, space and measurement both groups recorded scores at all levels from 0 to 3. However, as Figure 8.6 shows, there are slightly better scores for the Bookstart group. Although the Bookstart mean (1.4146, SD = 0.7062) is higher than the comparison group (1.1463, SD = 0.7267), the difference is not significant.

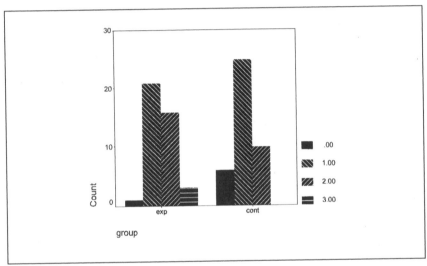

Figure 8.5 Number

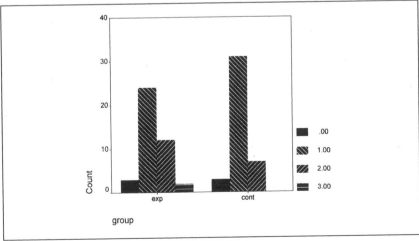

Figure 8.6 Shape, space, etc.

When the three English scores are taken together, highly significant differences between the two groups emerge (t = 2.929, p = < 0.01). At the extremes of the scale no Bookstart child obtains the lowest scores of 0 or 1 and no comparison group child scores the maximum of 9, or even 8. Figure 8.7 shows the differences in means between the groups: Bookstart 4.5854, SD = 1.7603; comparison 3.5122, SD = 1.5512.

A similar contrast occurs when the three mathematics scores are taken together, with the Bookstart group outperforming the other. At the extremes of the scale more Bookstart children score 7 or 8 and none scores 0. Figure 8.8 shows how the total mathematics mean of 4.4146 (SD = 1.932) for the Bookstart group compares with 3.5366 (SD = 1.9506) for the comparison group, a significant difference (t= 2.052, p = < 0.05).

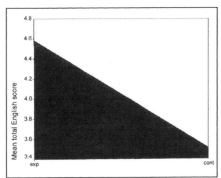

Figure 8.7

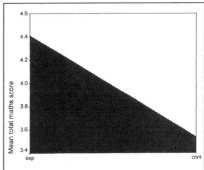

Figure 8.8

Finally, the overall total Baseline score gives a statistically significant (t = 2.52, p = < 0.05) difference between group means, as Fig. 8.9 shows. The Bookstart group mean of 9.000 (SD = 3.5071) compares with the comparison mean of 7.0732 (SD = 3.4161).

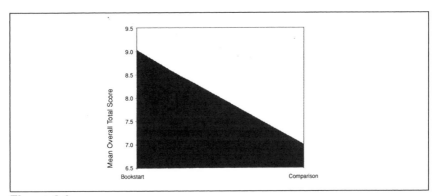

Figure 8.9

Discussion

The findings reported above are consistent and cumulative. On each of the six baseline assessments the Bookstart group records a higher range of scores than does the comparison group. The trend of these results indicates that the Bookstart group, who had all received the Bookstart pack in infancy, had been better prepared for school by their early childhood experiences. This conclusion is consistent with previous studies (Wade and Moore 1996a, b, 1997) using different samples which indicated that Bookstart children at age $2\frac{1}{2}$ to 3 had more experience with books, showed more interest in and concentration on books and engaged in more active book sharing with parents and carers.

While some of the individual assessments do not produce significant results, the cumulative score for English is highly significant and that for mathematics is significant, as is the combined Baseline score. Two individual assessments produce dramatic results. A difference in reading might have been predicted from the research findings reviewed above. In fact, the difference between groups turned out to be very highly significant. Similarly, if less predictably, the difference in number assessment was highly significant. Thus the superiority of the Bookstart sample is affirmed compared with a similar group who had not received the early advantage of book gifting. The fact that Bookstart children were further ahead in mathematics suggests that there may be pay-offs across the curriculum, not only in literacy.

The significance of higher scoring in Baseline Assessment should not be underestimated. It seems likely that an early start with books has provided the reciprocal interaction, experimentation, practice and motivation that lead to learning. Our findings reaffirm the central role that parents and carers play in the education of preschool children. We explicated this role above. Further, the findings corroborate research discussed above, particularly in underlining the relationship between reading achievement and early book sharing. Indications here are that early book sharing may lead to a general superiority as well as significantly establishing the foundations of literacy.

It is important to recall evidence (for example Wells 1986, Butler 1988, Juel 1988, Bus *et al.* 1995) that those children who are higher achievers at the onset of schooling maintain their position relative to other children as primary education continues. If Bookstart produces higher scoring in Baseline Assessment and such superiority is maintained, then it represents an extremely cost-effective way of promoting higher standards in literacy and possibly also across the curriculum.

We have already referred to the intriguing and unexpected superiority of the Bookstart group in mathematics. The large part of this superiority is gained through the highly significant difference in number assessment. Assessment of number focuses on counting. Thus for a score of 1 a child would need to demonstrate ability to count with objects up to 5 (for example, counting with fingers in a rhyming song). A score of 2 necessitates observation of the ability to recognise and count with objects and order numbers to at least 10 (for example counting and organising numbers to 10 and placing them in the correct sequence). For a score of 3 the child would require to be observed recognising, counting and writing numbers to at least 20 with a reasonable degree of accuracy.

The reasons for this marked superiority of Bookstart children in number require further investigation. Firstly, books are a learning resource and many books for young children introduce number and counting in interesting and interactive ways. Some stories focus directly on number and sequence: e.g. *Three Bears* and *Ten Nine Eight*. Then, too, early children's books contain number rhymes: e.g. *5 Little Ducks, 10 in a Bed* and *One, Two, Three, Four Five, Once I Caught a Fish Alive.* Repeated practice and interaction, say with finger rhymes when sharing books, are likely to make incidental number learning efficient and interesting.

A second possibility is that regular acts of book sharing in the preschool years encourage attention and concentration. Book sharing provides pleasurable and purposeful quality time for both infants and adults and we know that it is easier to concentrate if activities are purposeful. Our follow up observational studies (Wade and Moore 1996a, b, Moore and Wade 1997) showed this was so in book sharing in the home at about the age of three years. We regard attention and concentration as important for learning in all subject areas, not merely in the fields of oracy and literacy. The argument for attention and concentration is supported by Rowe (1995), who concluded, from a longitudinal study of 5,092 students in 92 schools in Australia, that reading at home has much more effect on attainment than do socio-economic variables. Rowe's study drew attention to attentiveness in the classroom as an important predictor of reading achievement and also showed the powerful effect that reading activity at home has on attentiveness. His conclusion is that there is:

> a positive carry-over effect between activities at home and behaviour in the classroom which is clearly in the interests of individual students and other students, as well as teachers. That is, these findings indicate that the opportunity to develop and practise attentiveness-demanding skills at home results in positive transference of similar skills to the classroom. (page 90)

It will be interesting to discover if these very positive findings are replicated with different and larger samples. The potential of Bookstart is huge, for all evaluations so far have been positive. One aspect is the potential to increase educational standards, particularly in the light of research referred to above that those children entering school with advantages retain their superiority after two years of schooling. A further potential of Bookstart is its ability to affect those 'hard to reach' families.

Recently Bookstart has attracted a national sponsor and with the administration of Book Trust the possibility exists to make Bookstart a national programme and the entitlement of every child. Certainly Bookstart is an important project in that it recognises the central role that parents and carers play in their children's intellectual, emotional and moral development. Stories and rhymes lay the foundation for literacy development and much else, including pleasure and quality time shared by adults and their children.

It follows that parents need to be alerted early on to both their own significant role and to the early learning potential of their preschool children. We have made a beginning in this direction (Wade and Moore 1999) and are delighted that this volume does too.

Acknowledgements

We are grateful for the support of the Unwin Charitable Trust and the Roald Dahl Foundation and acknowledge the use of some material previously printed in *Educational Review*.

References

Ainsworth, M. D. S. and Bell, S. M. (1970) Attachment, exploration and separation: illustrated by the behaviour of one year-olds in a strange situation, *Child Development* 41, pp. 50-67.

Appleton, T., Clifton, R. and Goldberg, S. (1975) 'The development of behavioural competency in infancy', in Horowitz, F. G. (ed.) *Review of Child Development Research*, Vol. 4. Chicago, Il: University of Chicago Press.

Birmingham City Council (1996) *Baseline Assessment for the Primary Phase*. Birmingham City Council and Focus in Education Productions.

Bower, T. G. R. (1979) *Human Development*. San Francisco, Calif.: Willi Freeman & Co.

Brice Heath, S. (1989) 'Oral and literate traditions among black Americans living in poverty', in Shann, P. (ed.) *Becoming Political: Readings and writings in the politics of literacy education*, 294. Portsmouth, NH: Heinemann.

Bronfenbrenner, V. (1979) *The Ecology of Human Development*. Cambridge, Mass.: Harvard University Press.

Bryant, P. and Bradley, L. (1985) *Children's Reading Problems*. Oxford: Blackwell.

Bus, A. G., Ijzendoorn, M. H. and Pellegrini, A. D. (1995) 'Joint book reading makes for success in learning to read: a meta-analysis on intergenerational transmission of literacy', *Review of Educational Research* **65**(1), 1–21.

Butler, S. R. (1988) 'Pre-school language processing performance and later reading achievement', in Masland, R. L. and Masland, M. W. (eds) *Preschool Prevention of Reading Failures*, 19–51. Parkton, Md.: York Press.

Debaryshe, B. D. (1993) 'Joint picture-book reading correlates early language skill', *Journal of Child language* **20**, 455–61.

Hannon, P. and James, S. (1990) 'Parents' and teachers' perspective on pre-school literacy development', *British Educational Research Journal*, **16**, 259–72.

Juel, C. (1988) 'Learning to read and write: a longitudinal study of 54 children from first through fourth grades', *Journal of Educational Psychology* **80**, 437–47.

Moore, M. and Wade, B. (1997) 'Parents and children sharing books: an observational study', *Signal*, September 203-14.

Piaget, J. (1952) *The Origins of Intelligence in Children*. New York: International University Press.

Piaget, J. (1954) *The Construction of Reality in the Child*. New York: Basic Books.

Richards, M. P. (1974) *The Integration of a Child into a Social World*. Cambridge: Cambridge University Press.

Rowe, K. J. (1995) 'Factors affecting students' progress in reading; key findings from a longitudinal study', *Literacy, Teaching and Learning* **1**, 57-110.

Scarborough. H. S. and Dobrich, W. (1994) 'On the efficacy of reading to pre-schoolers', *Developmental Review*, 245–302.

Toomey, D. (1993) 'Parents hearing their children read: a review. Rethinking the lessons of the Haringey Project', *Education Review* **35**, 223–36.

Wade, B. (1984) *Story at Home and School*. Educational Review Occasional Publication. Birmingham: University of Birmingham.

Wade, B. and Moore, M. (1993) *Bookstart*. London: Book Trust.

Wade, B. and Moore, M. (1996a) 'Home activities: the advent of literacy', *European Early Childhood Education Research Journal* **4**(2), 63–76.

Wade, B. and Moore, M. (1996b) 'Children's early book behaviour', *Educational Review* **48**, 283-8.

Wade, B. and Moore, M. (1999) *Baby Power*. Handforth: Egmont World.

Wells, G. (1985) *Language, Learning and Education*. Slough: NFER-Nelson.

Wells, G. (1986) *The Meaning Makers*. Portsmouth, NH: Heinemann.

Chapter 9

'Am I doing it right?' Share – a national parental involvement programme

Lisa Capper

Introduction

Every parent wants to know what their children are doing in school and how well they are doing. Many want to become more directly involved with their children's education by helping their child learn, but are not always sure of the best way of going about it. Invariably they ask the question 'Am I doing it right?' As professionals, it is often easy for us to think that we know what parents need, but parents are not a homogeneous group and there is not one simple recipe for success in involving parents in their children's learning.

Share is a school-based national parental involvement initiative launched in 1996 by CEDC (Community Education Development Centre), a national charitable trust. It offers a practical 'hands on' approach for primary schools to involve parents in their children's learning and aims to increase their cooperation and commitment at an early stage. Share offers parents an opportunity to gain accreditation for supporting their children in this way, delivered through the Open College Network. Teachers are trained in working with parents in a small group situation and in using the Share materials, which focus on literacy and numeracy (Share carrier bag, Share books, memo pad, pen and badge), and accreditation programme. Share has three aims:

- to improve the educational attainment of children;
- to motivate parents to take an active interest in their children's education and to further their own education;
- to develop effective management and organisation of parental involvement in schools.

Share takes a long-term approach with the model beginning in year one and growing up the school. Together, teachers, parents and children learn new skills, together with parents and children holding the learning materials firmly in their own hands. The results have led to:

- teacher confidence and skills in working with groups of adults;
- school recognition of the contribution of home school initiatives;
- understanding on the part of school inspectors about issues such as family and adult learning and accreditation;
- greater understanding of issues surrounding partnerships between home and school;
- working across boundaries, changing attitudes and achieving mutual respect.

Share was developed against the backdrop of the new Labour Government ideology – 'education for the many, not just the few' and relates to several policy areas such as school improvement with target-setting and baseline assessment, the raising standards agenda with emphasis on literacy and numeracy, home–school agreements and homework and government plans for lifelong learning. In a very short amount of time Share has penetrated about a quarter of all local authorities in England and created presence in Wales and Scotland and has generated a large body of new knowledge and experience of home–school work. Spin-offs for CEDC's Share Project include 'A Fair Chance' – a Share project for foster carers and young people looked after by local authorities, and 'It's a Man Thing' – a fathers and children literacy project.

'I never did very well in school. I wanted Joe to do much better, but I didn't know how to help until I started doing Share.' (Parent)

Background to Share

CEDC is a national charitable trust, which works towards improving access to learning, especially those who have benefited least from learning opportunities. Share is one of several national CEDC programmes which aim to practically demonstrate the effectiveness of a community-based learning approach in promoting social inclusion.

Social exclusion costs the community heavily – in the form of crime, poor health, dependency on benefits and social breakdown. People who are excluded, by definition fail to participate in decision-making, and in civil and cultural life. This is a tragic waste of potential. To achieve economic success, a modern society needs an adaptable, highly educated, healthy and skilled workforce. This means harnessing the abilities and creative potential of everyone in the workforce and in the community. Developing a culture of lifelong learning is central to this view (*A Fair Deal for Learning,* CEDC 1999) and to the Share project. There have been several government reports (Fryer 1997, Moser 1999) which advocate the necessity of locally available learning opportunities which offer variety, flexibility and which embrace diversity. Moser recommends every infant and primary school in disadvantaged areas should offer family literacy and numeracy projects by 2002.

Share is set against the background of the plethora of research, which argues that parental involvement in children's education can raise attainments and support the development of young children's learning (Tizard and Hughes 1984, Topping and Wolfendale 1985, Merttens and Morgan 1993). The context of the home, and the socio-economic status of the home environment, as a place of learning has also been explored as a determining factor in children's learning (National Commission on Education 1993), and the emerging formalisation of the relationship between home and school of the late 1990s is beginning to be scrutinised (Bastiani 1996), with issues such as parental choice, consultation, home–school agreements and homework policies at the fore.

The new area of work for which Share offers exploration is the recognition of parents as learners themselves in the home–school liaison process, the nature of their relationship with the school, and the impact of this approach on the child's learning. Although the children's learning in Share is focused on literacy and numeracy, the adult learning element is concerned with parents' knowledge and understanding of issues such as how children learn, study support, supporting their children's literacy and numeracy skills, the importance of home–school links and managing transition, together with practical skills such as making and using learning materials. This is strikingly different to the government sponsored Family Literacy and Numeracy programmes offered through the Basic Skills Agency which instead teaches basic skills to parents, uses a highly-structured plan and is a combination of both separate and joint provision for parents and pupils. Share also takes an important step away from the idea of the naive parent with child as instructor.

The Share family learning approach, with different learning opportunities for all involved, builds on the legacy of PACT shared reading (Hackney Local Education Authority (Bastiani and Wolfendale 1996)), IMPACT (University of North London) shared maths and writing, and on the range of local home-grown initiatives from around the country and packages it up for general consumption. The anchor is the set of principles, common to all CEDC's project work, which aim to promote schools as centres of learning for the community and promote learning as the change agent for communities.

Lifelong learning is central to the school effectiveness and improvement debate and is cited as a norm in this process by Stoll and Fink (1996). The inclusiveness of Share as a parental involvement model, it could be further argued, embraces the set of norms and extends the school improvement process into the home–school arena and ultimately into the home and community.

The Norms of Improving Schools

- Shared goals: 'We know where we're going.'
- Responsibility for success: 'We can succeed.'
- Collegiality: 'We're in this together.'
- Continuous improvement: 'We can get better.'
- Lifelong learning: 'Learning is for everyone.'
- Risk-taking: 'We learn by trying something new.'
- Support: 'There is always someone there to help.'
- Mutual respect: 'Everyone has something to offer.'
- Openness: 'We can discuss our differences.'
- Celebration and humour: 'We feel good about ourselves.'

The overarching vision of the 'Shareschool' with every parent supporting their children's learning, and the underlying principles of the project, has fired its swift and continuous development; Share is politically well-placed, linking in with and cited in key government policy documents relating to post-16 education, raising standards and school improvement, but most importantly, it is effective in enthusing both parents and children and is therefore attractive to schools; 'A project like Share provides a unique partnership for teachers and parents to focus on learning...It gives schools something to get hold of' (Primary Inspector).

From a pilot phase of 20 schools in five local education authorities, it has grown to 30 local authorities and over 350 schools (as of May 1999). Originally offered at Key Stage 1, Share now has a Key Stage 2 model and a development underway for a secondary school Share project for Key Stage 3. The roll-out programme is supported by the Share Approved Trainer route, enabling senior officers, inspectors, head teachers and local authority trainers to deliver the Share teacher training course at a local level with all its nuances.

The nuts and bolts of it

Share is now an established model, of parents, their children and teachers working together in a strong home–school teaching and learning triad. Groupwork was chosen as the preferred methodology for Share, as it enables the players, both parents and teachers, to achieve things which they might not be able to achieve alone and is less daunting to parents and teachers alike than a formal taught course. In the context of home–school it has other added attractions:

'the informality means I am not so nervous of getting it wrong' (parent)

'If you've got problems you find out in a group that you're not the only one and you can talk about it' (parent)

'They are all so supportive and we are all there for the same thing' (teacher)

'If you help them without a scheme like this you think "Am I doing it right?"' (parent)

'It's the best forty minutes of the week' (parent)

'The children have shown great pleasure about having their parents visit school regularly to talk about Share and meet in the staffroom – they appear to feel proud and pleased' (Head teacher)

Share continues to be an important feature in attracting and sustaining the interest of what might be regarded as 'hard to reach' parents. For teachers, the informal approach allows for a more relaxed style and an easy structure, requiring only a small amount of preparation once the group is established.

'The teachers who attend the Share training go away feeling they now have some tools to actually work closely with the parents on the work they are doing in class, and they continue to develop these skills as they run the project. More often than not the parents offer support to the teacher, and it is very much a joint effort.' (Project Worker)

Groupwork skills are owned by all participants, not just the class teacher; some Share groups have parent leaders and CEDC will be offering accreditation in the future for those parents organising or wishing to organise parent groups as part of the measures taken for developing sustainability of the project at a local level. There is a strong sense of Stoll's collegiality – 'we're in this together' and shared responsibility – 'we can succeed' (Stoll and Fink 1996).

The groupwork with parents and their consequent work at home with their child is supported by a set of Share materials. The Share books have a tried and tested parent-friendly design and all the activities, although linked to the National Curriculum and frameworks for literacy and numeracy, relate to the home and community environment rather than the classroom. One of the key roles for the teacher is demonstrating the links between classroom and community learning: 'The activities can really open their eyes to opportunities in everyday life, such as looking for things on walks and talking about home or finding shapes in the kitchen cupboard' (teacher). The large Share bag holds all the learning materials safe and the memo pad, pen and badge help build a sense of ownership and get parents started. Nor do teachers have to prepare material or reinvent the wheel: 'Everything is there ready to use and they're fun' (teacher). A great deal has been learnt in this project about writing activities for parents and children to use at home which offer more than the rather Gradgrind-type material available in the high street. The Share material contains features such as 'Skills used' telling parents what skills children have used in doing the activity, several help pages with clear and concise information on subjects such as records, National Curriculum, reading, special educational needs, and practical skills such as bookmaking. The 'key point' or 'point for parents' kicks off the activity with a piece of knowledge for the parent about the particular area of learning or why this activity is important. Indications of our success in this area is the reproduction of the Share-formatted pages in parents and teachers own work, the adoption of key ideas and emblems, not least the badger and the fact that many groups have developed their own ideas and adaptations as suggested within the material.

'One of the strengths of Share has been in developing parents' skills in spotting and tackling particular learning opportunities, through specially designed games and activities' (Bastiani, 1999). As this chapter is being written there are over 3,000 parents taking part in Share with many being involved for more than one year. Views of parents are particularly well recorded in the evaluation studies undertaken by CEDC (Bastiani 1999) and those of the school and local authorities. 'Playing games together helps so much, in that we both enjoy doing it. Most of the games help extend learning in reading, writing and maths and can be introduced in fun ways' (parent). 'Hayley looks forward to the special time we spend together when we are doing Share work, which is also fun' (parent). It is clear parents who are or have taken part in Share value the one to one time the project affords with their children and have renewed enthusiasm for their own learning. Parents and teachers have begun to appreciate the differing roles of school, home and family in supporting children's learning and recognise that supporting learning at home has benefits for personal and family relationships. (See Figures 9.1, 9.2, 9.3.)

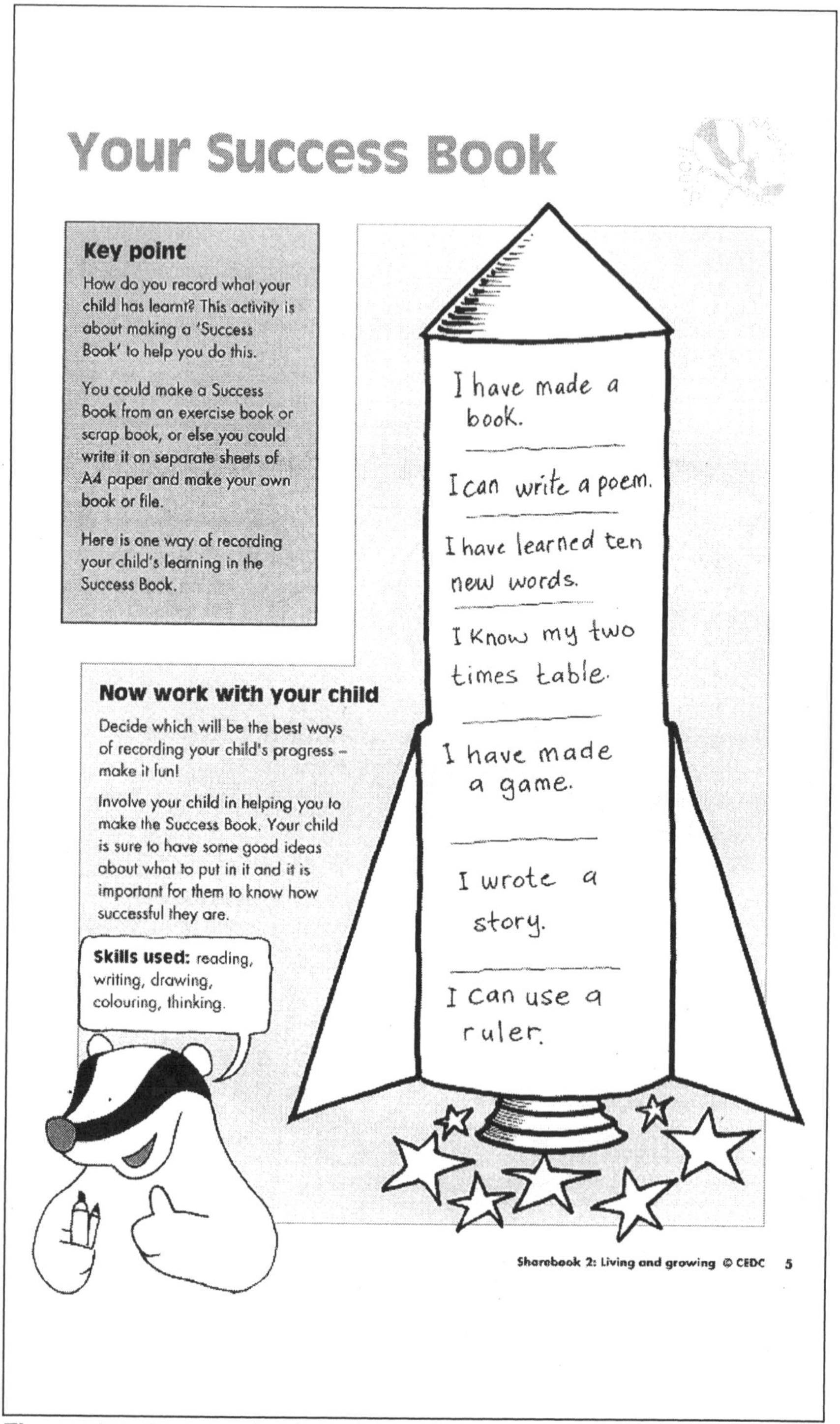

Your Success Book

Key point

How do you record what your child has learnt? This activity is about making a 'Success Book' to help you do this.

You could make a Success Book from an exercise book or scrap book, or else you could write it on separate sheets of A4 paper and make your own book or file.

Here is one way of recording your child's learning in the Success Book.

Now work with your child

Decide which will be the best ways of recording your child's progress – make it fun!

Involve your child in helping you to make the Success Book. Your child is sure to have some good ideas about what to put in it and it is important for them to know how successful they are.

Skills used: reading, writing, drawing, colouring, thinking.

Sharebook 2: Living and growing © CEDC 5

Figure 9.1 Success book activity, *Sharebook 2 Living and Growing* (CEDC 1997)

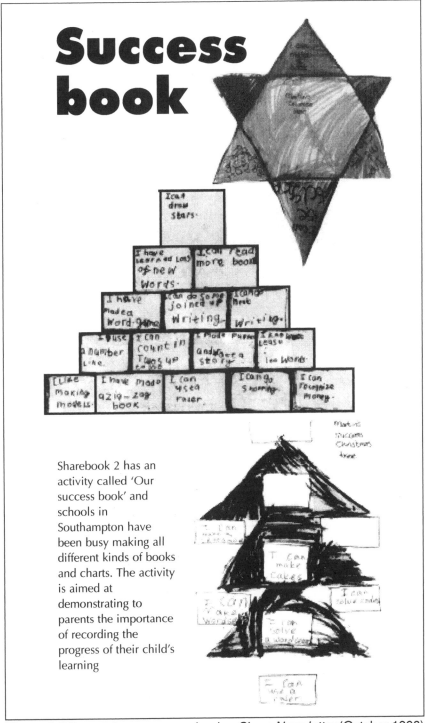

Figure 9.2 Parents' own success books, *Share Newsletter* (October 1998)

All About Me

KEY POINT
Carers, parents, teachers need to talk with children so that they can find out what children know and understand and what they can do.

NOW WORK WITH YOUR CHILD

Talk with your child and start to make a book together

Look at the front cover together. Read the title.

Find a photograph to put on the front cover or ask your child to draw a picture of themselves. Complete the cover by writing the name.

Talk about the first page of the book with your child.

Read it through together
Think about each section and complete using writing and pictures.

Now make a second page about your child using some of the ideas that you may have talked about e.g. their favourite things - toys, food, drink etc

KEY POINT - Encourage the children to talk confidently about themselves by responding positively. Praise what they can do and help them with what they are unable to do.

Skills used
thinking, writing, drawing, decision making, talking + listening

Figure 9.3 Parents' own activity 'All about me', *Share Newsletter* (October 1998)

Without 'fly-on-the-wall' documentary techniques it is always very hard to determine the actual practice taking place at home; most of the evidence to support the value of the Share home experience is drawn from Share group sessions, parents' diaries and the work the children produce at home. A recent example of a parent and pupil initiated activity is a booklet produced by mother and child entitled 'My community' which draws on three Share Key Stage 1 activities based on mapping the local area, identifying significant people and places and listing the learning partners supporting the child. Although the piece of work had been structured by the parent, the child had come up with the ideas for who to visit including the doctor, the police and the hospital where his baby sister was a regular visitor. The child had begun writing the text and mum had finished it off when the child had done enough (Figure 9.4); later in their book the reverse happens. The child had also taken some of the photographs.

The following extract demonstrates how the activities draw attention to specific numeracy skills while making the learning relevant, useful and fun. Starting from points of success with activities which parents are familiar with, such as Shopping is another feature of the material at all Key Stages.

> Made a shopping list out, working on his letter formation. He worked on lined paper but I added a line in the middle so he knew where to start with lower case words. We made a list of his favourite meal: Beans on toast, butter, yoghurt, Lemon Quosh. We talked about the different brands he could buy and to look out for any special offers. Also showed him money off coupons. I asked him to weigh me some fruit. We talked about sell-by dates. You can keep baked beans unopened for about 1 year. I explained bread would not last long. We left a slice of bread out to show him how long it would be before it went mouldy. We looked over last week's till receipt, seeing things itemized and all the different prices. This helped with his number recognition. I explained about corner shops having price stamps and big shops having bar codes. We found things in the cupboard that had bar codes and explained how it worked and how smaller shops had prices stamped on and would probably be more expensive. Liam crossed the items off the list as he went along. (Parent's diary, Warwickshire)

For parents whose children are at Key Stage 2, there are a whole new set of issues to be considered for home–school liaison work. There is sometimes less physical contact between parents and school as parents no longer take and collect their children. If parents have not been involved with their children's learning in the early years there are more barriers to break through and in terms of the Share model the complexity of the curriculum and the depth of knowledge required

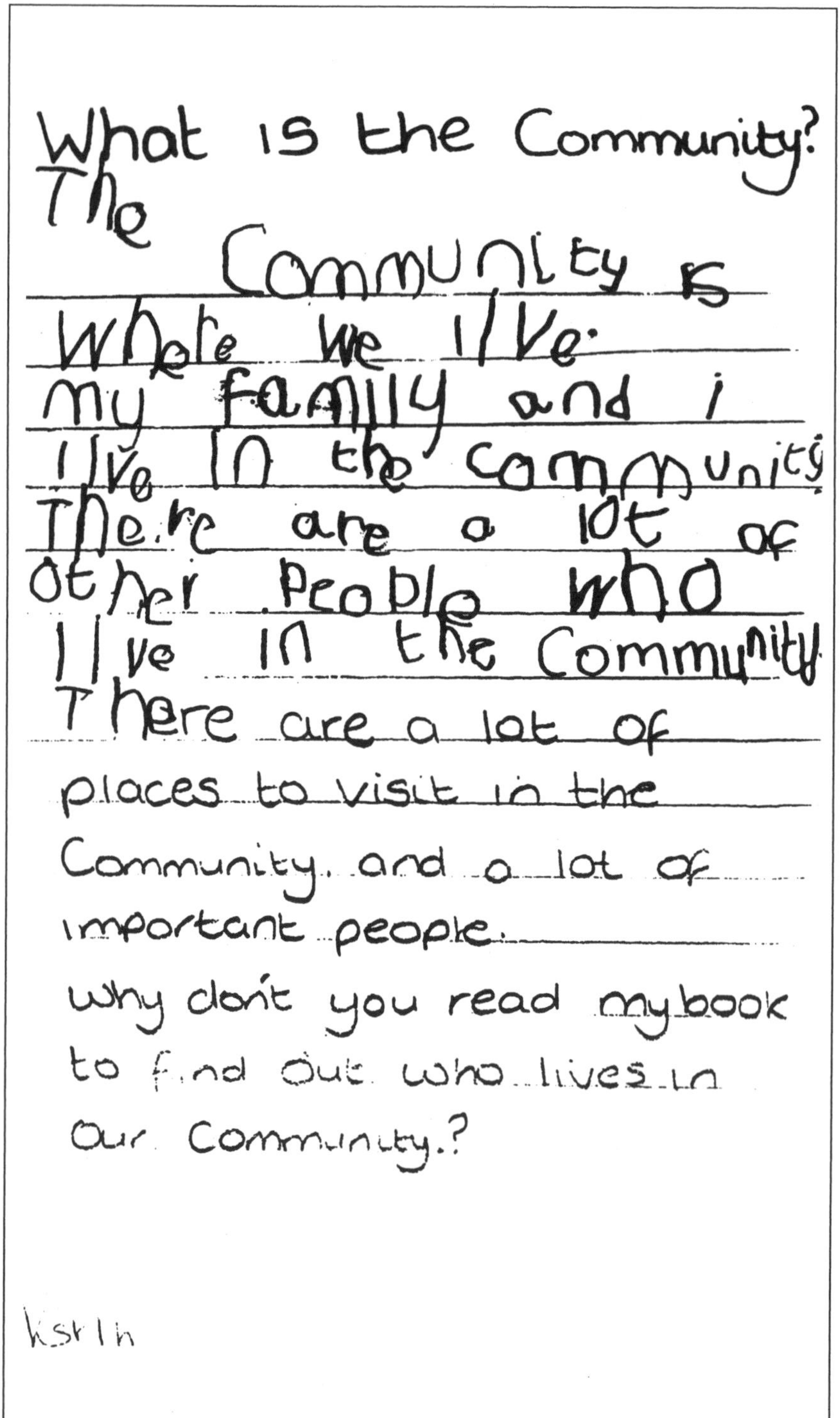

What is the Community?
The
           Community is
Where we live.
my family and i
live in the community
There are a lot of
other People who
live in the Community.
There are a lot of
places to visit in the
Community. and a lot of
important people.
why don't you read my book
to find out who lives in
Our Community.?

kst l h

Figure 9.4 'My Community' booklet

makes devising and using activities more challenging. Often, the teacher has a slightly more demanding role in explaining and demonstrating the activity. But for parents who have already been involved in Share, they are hungry for more and show great confidence in having a go. At a recent group meeting in Leicester, I witnessed a Key Stage 2 Share group that was looking at two activities. 'Lots of letters' is an activity which focuses on collecting, tallying and presenting data and focuses on the frequency of occurrence of different alphabet letters in written English. The parents had come up with other ideas for the activity including looking at the collection of coloured bottles in the bathroom. 'Could they use tins from the cupboard', one parent asked. 'There may not be enough variety,' said another. 'What about football? said another. The team or the scores?' 'Yes, he'd love that,' said the parent. Meal Maths is an activity which uses takeaway menus as a focus for addition and subtraction of money quantities. One parent told me that when the menu for a new take away was put through the door they could compare it to their regular one – 'what a bargain!' she told me. Not only are the parents and teacher in this situation involved in risk taking ('we learn by trying something new'), they are engaged in continually extending and improving their understanding of the activities and the associated learning – 'we can get better'.

Letters don't work

At its inception, Share set out 'to meet the needs of all parents' (OFSTED 1997) but especially those who for one reason or another had benefited least from learning. The starting point for Share teachers in training is to examine the possible barriers to parental involvement and to find the most appropriate method for recruitment from the suggested range. Many of the obstacles derive from parents' previous negative experience of education, their background or circumstances, for example, refugees, cultural and/or linguistic diversity, lifestyle, disaffection and related issues of confidence and self esteem.

> 'We knew that letters were often not an effective means of communicating with home. Parents who could read often did not read them, and some had reading difficulties that prevented them getting information from letters. We decided instead to approach parents either singly or in small groups.' (teacher)

For all schools, attempting to meet the OFSTED criteria, including 'hard-to-reach' groups effectively and over time is challenging. Share at least provides a philosophy, a structure, materials and an approach that promotes flexibility and adaptability and is staffed by teachers who have had their awareness raised even if they have not wholeheartedly adopted its principles.

'The structure of Share, with its informal groupwork and Share activities, gives some parents a second chance to get involved at a level and pace which suits them' (Deputy head teacher)

It is easy to pick out distinct examples where Share is meeting the needs of specific groups, for example, linguistically diverse groups, travellers, fathers, deaf parents and parents with a basic skills need.

'I do realise that it is important for us to help the children. I am thinking about these things more and more.' (Parent, Traveller Education Service (Wakefield), Bastiani 1999)

As the following two examples (from Bastiani 1999) show, Share has displayed spectacular success in working with linguistically diverse groups in multicultural schools. In spite of surface similarities, however, the two examples are different.

Example 1: Southwark

In this group, the overwhelming majority of parents were born in other countries and experienced schooling there. (One of the things they made together was a collage incorporating the eight flags of their countries of origin!) Their common language, however, was English; they all spoke it as their second language, and it was often used in the home. Interestingly, the very energetic and talented teacher was herself a multilingual member of an ethnic minority. The group enjoyed almost 100 per cent attendance and most members gained accreditation for their work.

Example 2: Leicester

In this multicultural school, most of the pupils come from Gujarati, Hindi or Punjabi speaking families. The commitment of the school to Share, combined with the specialist knowledge, skill and experience of ABE (Adult Basic Education) and bilingual support staff, turned a situation of mind-blowing linguistic complexity into a positive resource from which everyone – parents, staff and pupils – could benefit.

For example, parents completed Share comments in their workbooks in a variety of ways:

- in their own mother tongue
- in English, as their second language
- with English translations provided by
  - themselves
  - other group members
- with the help of a member of the Share team, with an appropriate language background
- helped by other members of their family.

'Most importantly, for a school such as ours, parents realised that a lack of English language doesn't mean that parents are unable to support their children's education...The input of the parents' first language, whilst reading and telling stories, gave children a richer diversity of language skills.' (HSL Coordinator)

But equally, if not more challenging, is where Share schools are working with a wide range of need and ability and a mixture of background and expectations. Here potential difficulties such as parents' comparison of children's work, the availability of resources within the family, the level of interaction in the group, the introduction, presentation and use of materials and attendance levels all become significant. Keeping the 'hard-to-reach' parents in this situation is paramount if Share is to be wholly inclusive. The skills of the Share teacher and head teacher in relating to and communicating with parents is of great importance in working in this very typical environment. Working towards a culture in school where staff, parents and pupils recognise that everyone has something to offer and where differences can be discussed should be a wider aim for the improving school and within that, the Share project. One such mixed catchment school devised the following code for its now three Share teachers.

Techniques for keeping parents who are 'hard to get to'

- Link Share to classwork and individual children's needs.
- Increase parents' awareness of the importance of Share.
- Keep people in touch – send information home, telephone.
- Ensure that each person can contribute.
- Value the contributions people make.
- Listen to parents' reasons for not attending. Act on them if appropriate – for example, problems over childcare, or not having done tasks during the week.
- Use other initiatives to encourage continued involvement, such as displays and workshops.
- Put up displays of work done by the Share group.
- Ensure that people keep to the ground rules for working in the group.

(Extract from Share teachers' presentation, April 1997, CEDC *Share Teachers' Handbook*)

Feeling good about learning

Share has a purpose-built accreditation programme for parents, delivered via the Open College Network, which focuses on the whole process of supporting children's learning at Key Stages 1 and 2 covering topics such as understanding home–school links, how children learn, study support, transition and there is a special research project for parents who want to do more without their child. This is a comprehensive programme, built into the Share project materials, and flexible enough to allow all parents to receive an annual award even if they have basic skills needs. Uniquely, it is the class teacher, in partnership with adult and community education services or its equivalent, who support the parents as part of the group activity. Like all new models, there was initial resistance to the idea of offering this opportunity through the primary school: 'The accreditation thing came as a shock to me. It's one thing working with children, quite another working with parents' (teacher). There are a number of interrelated reasons why such a feature was introduced to the project design: first was the importance of trying to break the cycles of underachievement that occur in families by introducing a structured learning element for parents; second, the primary school offered an easily accessible route for under-confident parents to return to learning, and third, to introduce learning as a firm feature of the home-learning culture through providing positive adult role models.

Now in its third year of operation, the full outcomes of this aspect of the work are still emerging. One such important outcome is the developing vision of Share schools that are beginning to recognise the crucially important task of teaching pupils within the context of their family and community.

> 'Many of our parents have been alienated from the education process. This could be the pathway back into the education system which would enable some to fulfill their potential alongside that of their children.' (Deputy head teacher)

After just twelve months Bastiani reports, 'There has been an important shift in the nature of teachers' concern about accreditation, away from issues of principle and approach and towards issues of training and support' (Bastiani 1999).

Many teachers have recognised the attractiveness of the accreditation programme as a structure for their work with parents (see Figure 9.5), whether or not they choose to go forward with formal accreditation; the 'shared goals' (Stoll and Fink 1996). Currently, at least 50 per cent of Share parents go through the accreditation process each year. There are clear benefits to parents in terms of both personal development and progression routes and schools continue to report a steady number of parents who carry on succeeding. There are examples of parents going on to college, studying for National Vocational Qualifications, gaining employment, making applications for jobs, being promoted. Schools have seen a spin-off for themselves with Share parents becoming volunteers, training as classroom assistants, becoming parent governors and of course, gains in children's behaviour and learning. 'Last year I would never have dreamed I could work with my son at home like I have, let alone put myself forward to do an NVQ course. Share has given me loads of confidence and shown me I can do things other people do' (parent). A father at an awards event at the Town Hall said privately to me 'This is the only certificate I've ever had in my life and my daughter helped me get it.'

One key area left for investigation, which the formal evaluation report (Bastiani, 1999) does not cover, is the impact of the parents' accredited learning, in this formalised sense, on the child. In practice and on an anecdotal level, it is easy to see the benefits; children looking proudly on as Mum or Dad receive their award, conversation between child and peer group and between child and teacher about this experience, joint ownership of the 'Share file'. Many teachers have commented on the shared confidence and self-esteem of parent and child; but which elements of Share contribute to this? Celebration of learning? Taking responsibility for learning? Risk taking? Shared goals? Shared knowledge and skills? Parent mediation – 'What the child can do in cooperation today, he can do alone tomorrow' (Vygotsky 1962).

D1 **Learning Together:** Home, school & community
To support early reading, writing & mathematics

D2 **Credit Level: Level One**   D3 **Credit Value: 2**

D4 **Learning Outcomes:**	D5 **Assessment Criteria**
By the end of this unit learners will:	The learner has achieved the learning outcomes because s/he can:
1 Be able to recognise that opportunities exist in the home and community to support early reading, writing and mathematics.	1 Identify four different ways to learn in the home and four in the community.
2 Understand the importance of shared learning or 'quality time' to foster learning.	2 Identify four features of shared learning and give reasons why they are important in helping children learn.
3 Develop an understanding of equal opportunities issues relevant to home and community learning.	3 Identify and describe four ways that learning can help at home.
4 Understand that grandparents, parents and children learning together has special features.	4 List four advantages of children, parents and grandparents learning together.

Figure 9.5 Extract from the Share Accreditation Programme

The impact of Share on pupil progress

To evaluate Share solely in terms of its contribution to pupil progress is to miss half the story. Already, in this short account, it will be clear to the reader that Share has wider and lasting benefits for parents, pupils, teachers, schools and other agencies. 'The Share approach often leads to permanently changed behaviour and relationships, which have continuing and cumulative advantages for all those involved' (Bastiani 1999). There is no doubt that Share contributes to the raising standards agenda and from the beginning of its life has had to prove its existence on these terms. The evaluation study (Bastiani 1999) exposes the issues surrounding such a task such as the difficulties of reliability in measuring family influences, the validity of methods used to collect data in the absence of standardised testing and the need to support crude hard data with qualitative information. The result is a report that convincingly draws on a combination of evidence to demonstrate progress.

> At the beginning of the project I recorded how many Keywords the children knew; their writing and reading statement banks; number recognition and number bonds. When looking at progress, I compared Share children with an equivalent child in their class group. All children had improved their Keywords. The Share children had improved between 5 words and 93 more words, the average being around 20–22 more words. The Share children in the lower class group seemed to have learnt more words than the others in that group. The Share children in the middle and top groups seemed to be on a par with their peers.
>
> Writing progress was generally on a par with other members of the class, although the Share children show more confidence and are more willing to have a go at independent writing.
>
> Number skills have increased with Share children generally on a par with peers, but three boys are working with numbers over 100 whereas they were only working with numbers up to 10 in January. Other children in their group are only working with numbers to 20. These parents have been working on activities mainly to do with number and I feel it is this extra work with Share that has increased their confidence and enthusiasm for numbers. (Teacher, Birmingham, Bastiani 1999)

Parents have kept their own records and diaries '29.10.96 – Liam now knows 55 words (from 100 Common Words list). He has learnt 11 new words since we started working together. 7.3.97 – Liam got 90 words this week on his list. I am really pleased with him. He has done really well. He was the one that suggested that we do them. I usually have to encourage him. Share project this week is a progress chart. We are making an A3 poster. Liam has used the ruler to divide it into 4. One Maths – English – Science and Swimming. The first one we did was English, 100 common words.'

Share children throughout the scheme are encouraged to plan and review their own work, organise parts of their learning at home, create and contribute to their own records and develop and use rules and boundaries.

One very significant aspect of Share is the emphasis on 'Learning Together' which is also the title of the first Share book and accreditation unit. The development of this activity preceded the Government's legislation for home–school agreements and homework policies and features within the pages of its guidance. Share sees a range of agreements at different levels; between the parents and pupil (Working Well and Success Story activities), the teacher and parents (Play by the rules) and CEDC, the LEA and school (Quality learning certificate). The 'Learning Together Rules' (see Figure 9.6) from the 'Working Well' activity at Key Stage 1 and reiterated in 'Success Story' at Key Stage 2 have been used effectively throughout Share schools and not just in the year group which has adopted the Share project.

They have successfully set up the conditions and relationships needed to capitalise on the benefits of the home–school relationship and offer an agreement that is firmly held in the hands of families.

Essential ingredients for Share as a school effectiveness tool

There are few instances where schools have not made a success of Share, mainly due to the flexibility afforded by its simple design and strong underpinning values. In the very few cases where it has stopped or never got off the ground, it is usually as a result of fundamental issues relevant to the whole school as well as the Share model. Issues to watch out for include the unforgivable and the unavoidable; changes of staff disrupt groupwork activity; Share materials often need 'interpreting' for parents, more so at the level of Key Stage 2. Where parents have a basic skills need or speak other languages, extra resource and support is needed. Leadership from the head teacher and ultimately the local authority is needed to maintain the status and profile of Share and other work with parents. As always, time and money plague the evaluation returns at every corner. The evidence so far predicts the following ingredients for the successful implementation of Share.

- Family learning is a now a central plank in the Government's raising standards and lifelong learning agenda. Share offers a tried and tested model to support schools in improving their work in both of these areas. The essential ingredients for success in using

Figure 9.6 Share rules

the Share model rely on schools extending their improvement plan to families and communities.

- Shared goals; recognition of the part parents can play in school improvement and pupil progress.
- Collegiality; between staff, parents, pupil and other key agencies such as adult education, community education and accrediting bodies, working in partnership with other Share schools.

- Mutual respect; the needs of parents and pupils are considered and met on an equal basis to the needs of the school; inclusive recruitment and retention strategies, meeting the needs of children in the care system.
- Learning triad; class teacher working with parents and pupils, links to work in class; head teacher support essential.
- Lifelong learning; to recognise parents as learners themselves, to see the school as the centre of learning in the community, to accompany Share with a programme of professional development for teachers – teachers must be learners, too.
- Recognising progress; systems for monitoring and evaluating and publicising success.
- Celebration; feeling good about learning.
- Resources; space and time for parents and relocation of resources into the home.
- Risk taking; trying something new, continually improving practice.
- Whole–school approach to working with parents and families; openness and support from day one.

For those schools that are still in the mindset of thinking that parents 'won't come', then think again!

Share

Today is Wednesday and its time for
Share
Plenty turned up for the meeting
there
We would like to thank you for inventing
Share
It's nice to know that someone
cares
We need your help to show us the way it's
done,
To help our children and to make it
fun
Let's hope it stays for years to
come
Give the same chance to Everyone

(Extract from a longer poem by parents in Caerphilly 1999)

References

Bastiani, J. (1996) 'Home–school contracts and agreements – opportunity or threat?', in *Home–school Agreements*. London: RSA.

Bastiani, J. (1999) *An Evaluation of the First Two Years*. Coventry: Share, CEDC.

Bastiani, J. and Wolfendale, S. (1996) *Home–school Work in Britain*. London: David Fulton Publishers.

CEDC (1997) *Sharebook 2 Living and Growing*. Coventry: CEDC.

CEDC (1998) *Share Newsletter,* October.

CEDC (1999) *A Fair Deal For Learning*. Coventry: CEDC.

Fryer, R. H. (1997) *Learning for the Twenty-first Century. First report of the national advisory Group for Continuing Education and Lifelong Learning*. Suffolk: DfEE Publications.

Merttens, R. and Morgan, C. (1993) 'Parental involvement in Mathematics: the home as a social factor', in *Proceedings of the 1993 International Conference on Misconceptions in Science and Mathematics*. Cornell University Press.

Moser, (1999) *A Fresh Start – Improving literacy and numeracy*. Suffolk: DfEE Publications.

National Commission on Education (1993) *The Paul Hamlyn Report*.

OFSTED (1997) *Inspection and Re-inspection of Schools from September 1997: New requirements and guidance on their implementation*. London: OFSTED.

Stoll, L. and Fink, D. (1996) *Changing Our Schools: Linking school effectiveness and school improvement*. Buckingham: Open University Press.

Tizard, B. and Hughes, M. (1984) *Young Children Learning*. London: Fontana.

Topping, K. and Wolfendale, S. (1985) *Parental Involvement in Reading*. London: Croom Helm.

Vygotsky, L. (1962) translation of Hanfmann, E. and Vaker, G. *Thought and Language*. Cambridge, Mass.: MIT Press.

Other projects

Impact Maths and Shared Writing, University of North London, 166–220 Holloway Road, London N7 8DB. Contact Lin Taylor, telephone 020 7753 7052.

A Fair Chance – Learning Together, Supporting the educational achievements of children and young people in the care system, CEDC, Woodway Park School, Wigston Road, Coventry CV2 2RH. Contact Lisa Capper, telephone 01203 655700

'It's a Man Thing!' – fathers and reading project, CEDC, Woodway Park School, Wigston Road, Coventry CV2 2RH. Contact Lisa Capper, telephone 01203 655700.

BSA (Family literacy and numeracy project), Basic Skills Agency.

House, 1-19 New Oxford Street, London WC1A 1NU. Contact Annabel Hemstedt, telephone 0171 405 4017.

Chapter 10

ICT as a catalyst – parental involvement in the National Literacy Association Docklands Learning Acceleration Project

Ray Barker and Glen Franklin

The background

The London Docklands has long been seen as an area of business confidence and affluence. The towering presence of Canary Wharf has become a symbol of prosperity as the international base for major banks, newspapers and TV companies. However, the Docklands area is in the main, composed of three local authorities, Tower Hamlets, Newham and Southwark, all of which contain areas of severe urban deprivation and in terms of educational league tables have some of the lowest educational achievement and school attendance records in the country.

It was in the light of this underachievement that the London Docklands Development Corporation (LDDC) – the body set up in 1981 to regenerate the entire area – came together with the National Literacy Association (NLA) to develop, what was at the time, the biggest literacy and technology intervention in the UK. A part of the brief of the LDDC was to improve the scope for employment in London Docklands, thus encouraging companies to site themselves within its remit area. They realised that an important way of doing this was to work closely with schools to raise basic standards of literacy among Docklands residents, to give London Docklands children a good foundation on which to build the achievement of the rest of their employable lives. Something needed to be done; much had been attempted previously in the area, but not by an urban regeneration body.

In keeping with their mission of regeneration and innovation the LDDC and NLA put forward a proposal for a project driven by information and communications technology (ICT). This was to cost in the region of £1 million but would create a technological infrastructure within Docklands' schools which would last for years, change practice and ways of thinking to involve parents as partners in raising achievement, as well as making literacy an issue for the entire community. This chapter shows how the NLA Docklands Project raised pupil achievement by using this 'new' technology, to involve parents and carers in a 'new' way. With no precedent for such an intervention, all members of the partnership – pupils, teachers, schools, community – started without preconceptions. The NLA provided a change of approach, but built this around tried and tested ideas: the 'new' was built on 'traditional' foundations.

The National Literacy Association Docklands Learning Acceleration Project

This comprised:

- A two-year project aiming to improve standards of literacy and basic skills in 600 Year 3 children in 15 schools (including one special school);
- Using the latest developments in multimedia and portable technology to motivate children at school and to involve their families at home;
- Focusing on Integrated Learning Systems *Global English* software for the National Curriculum in school and Acorn PocketBook computers for home and school.

How would the Project carry out its aims?

The Project would:

- ensure the provision of daily sessions of *Integrated Learning Systems* English so that a sound foundation of basic reading and spelling skills is achieved;
- promote a wide range of activities to support literacy, e.g. differentiated homework, drama, group work, poetry workshops, paired and cooperative learning and produce resources to support these;
- use class sets of Acorn PocketBook computers with appropriate software to encourage child/parent partnership in the home;
- work with parent and community groups to engender positive and supportive attitudes towards the acquisition of literacy;
- support and train adults involved with children in the Project.

The Project team was clear that:

- This was not an 'ICT project' as such. It was to use technology as a part of what it was doing.
- It was to be externally evaluated.

- Team members would work closely with the 600 children and their families. The model was one of support and training on site.
- The Project would not follow any one implementation model, nor recommend any one approach.
- An aim would be to evaluate the many models in use and to offer suggestions as to reasons for success. Such models and expertise could then be disseminated to other areas in the country.

The National Literacy Association had long been advocating an educational target of 99 per cent literacy and had been involved with Ernst and Young (1993) in producing its seminal report to show the impact of literacy, education and training on the UK economy. This report showed that 60 per cent of all jobs required 'reasonable reading skills'. The report estimated the costs to the country of illiteracy, lost business, remedial education, crime and benefit payments to be over £10 million.

The NLA in its 'Pledge for Literacy' (1998) stated:

It is surely unacceptable for a child to be allowed to enter the fast-moving, intolerant, adult world of the 21st century without the skills to survive in it? *The National Literacy Association* believes that all children want to and *can* learn – some just need a little more help to do so! If you expect children to fail, they will have no faith in their own ability. Expect them to achieve and they will strive for success.

UNESCO states that it is the right of every child to be educated to the maximum of their potential. The NLA believes that it is the right of every child to acquire basic literacy – to be able to communicate with ease and confidence in whatever medium is required to affect that communication – whether it be reading, writing, speaking or sending an E-mail. Without literacy, each child is denied access to core skills necessary for learning and living; without literacy children cannot prepare themselves for a social, civic and economic role in the new millennium.

The model

This credo was central to the model created by the Project team.

Many researchers have shown what makes schools effective places for learning, and the team knew they needed to look closely at this work as they were dealing with the management of change in Project schools. Simply introducing something 'new', i.e. the technology, would not work. It would of course create more problems of management for teachers in a time of curriculum change. This is not a criticism of teachers or schools. Teachers are not necessarily rejecting change, they are merely posing important questions. The team knew they had to work holistically (see Figure 10.1) in order to affect all stakeholders in the educational process. Both Jaap

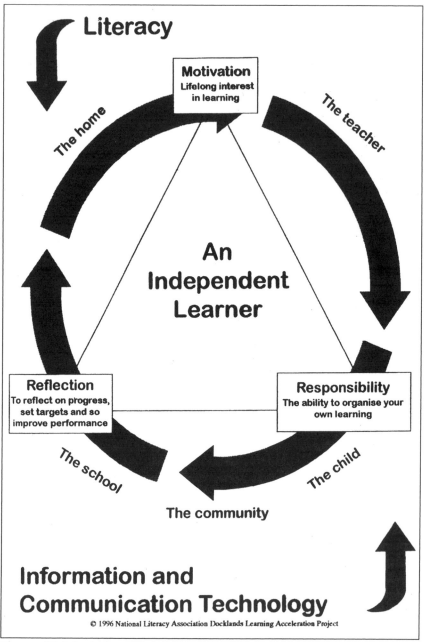

Figure 10.1 An Independent Learner

Scheerens (1992) and Mortimore *et al.* in School Matters (1988) commented on parental involvement being related to effective schools. Examples they quoted of such parental involvement included supporting pupils' educational development at home, assisting where possible in schools and attending parents meetings.

Studies have shown (Smith 1968, Walberg *et al.* 1980) that the academic performance of children increases when schools seek the assistance of parents and carers and directly support and involve them in supporting school learning. It is not sufficient simply to suggest what parents and carers can do with their children at home. They have the will – but not 'the way'. Dauber and Epstein (1989) showed that parents in an inner-city school wanted teachers to help them help their children at home and give them more information about the curriculum. Parents want to help their children. They just do not know the best way to do it. Or, in areas such as the East End of London, there may not be time, space or the resources to ensure parental involvement. It has been shown that many parents and carers doubt their own ability to help their children but still talk about wanting to help. More disturbingly, parents often say that their children's homework is beyond them, even when they do want to help (Leitch and Tangri 1988). Many parents do not enjoy coming into school. This is often because of their own bad experiences. They can feel intimidated by the place and the people in it. Often their only communication with the school concerns negative information about behaviour or attendance. Davies (1989) reported that a majority of such parents were surprisingly satisfied with their children's school work even though their children were obviously not being successful, which brings into question the whole issue of high expectations influencing performance in schools.

Ysseldyke and Christenson (1993) quote Rankin (1967), who worked with high achievers in Detroit schools. He found their parents provided experiences for them, talked to them about their work, helped with homework, showed interest in school work and took the initiative to contact teachers.

These were exactly the kinds of behaviours which we believed the input of ICT (the C does, after all, stand for 'communication') would provide. It was 'new', it was 'different', everyone was feeling insecure about the use of technology. For once, teachers, schools, parents and carers found themselves on a level playing field. The children had no such problems when using technology. They became the 'experts'; they found themselves in control, for once.

Using technology did not represent a pedagogical threat to the teacher. One thread running through research (Snider 1990, Epstein 1987) is that parents do have a role in educating their children but it is often difficult for teachers to acknowledge this. Often parental involvement in schools creates an awkward situation (Chavkin and Williams 1985). Using technology in school and at home removed the 'threat' and indeed created an extra impetus for parental support and involvement. In fact research is now showing (Vollands et al. 1999) how ICT can easily provide information on children's performance in literacy which can help teachers and parents alike to target areas of educational concern. They can work together to improve literacy.

The results

After two years of testing and discussion with children, teachers and the community, the London University Institute of Education produced its report on the Project. Key findings were:

1. In 1995, while the average age of the children involved was 7 years, 6 months, the average reading age was 6 years, 8 months.
2. By 1997, the average reading age had improved to 8 years, 8 months – i.e. the children had sustained reading gains of 12 months in one year, the national average.
3. In 1995, one school out of 15 was reading at national average. Two years later, ten schools were at or above the national average.
4. While issues such as socio-economic status and ethnicity are important considerations, they should not give rise to an expectation of underachievement:
5. progress in reading was not significantly influenced by whether a child received free school meals;
6. children from different ethnic backgrounds achieved similar rates of progress in both spelling and reading;
7. in 1997, children for whom English was an additional language did better in both reading and spelling than native speakers, significantly so in spelling.
8. In 1995 boys and girls were working at similar levels, but in 1996 girls were making significantly more progress than boys.

The really signifciant issue for the NLA was that inner-city children were shown as more than capable of progressing at national average levels. There was no reason for underachievement of these children if they could be helped.

It is also interesting that socio-economic status and ethnicity did not appear to make a difference in the improvements noted. These two factors have long been use as 'excuses' for the underachievement of children in inner-city schools. Although socio-economic status is an important predictor of student achievement (Mortimore *et al.* 1988) it is not the sole determinant as Milne (1989) and Davies (1989) have shown in the USA. So, what is it about using technology that acts as a 'leveller'?

The evaluation report of the NLA Docklands Learning Acceleration Project concluded:

Parental involvement in changing the culture of teaching and learning in inner city schools is an important ingredient. The project undoubtedly contributed to its encouragement and the most successful schools were the ones which harnessed parental support most effectively. The project team also contributed in various ways to raising literacy standards by supporting work in the communities from which the children came. In other words, community and parental involvement in the schooling of the inner city is an important factor in raising standards of achievement. This was amply demonstrated in the work of the project. (Scott *et al.* 1997, page 55)

So how did this happen? What is so particular about technology that it can enable or empower parents and carers to become involved in their children's school life and help children to improve so noticeably? Seymour Pappert (1993 and 1996) forecast massive change with the advent of technology in the home and school:

> I predict that this [technology] will create a force altering the structure, nature and content of schooling...Make allies of parents; an increasing number of parents are becoming critical and are unhappy. Try to develop a political base in the politics of the school. (Quotation from TES Online 18 September 1998).

In this vision, ICT becomes the catalyst for real change.

PocketBooks in the Docklands Learning Acceleration Project: a case study

Nicholas was seven years old and did not like writing; he did not see himself as a writer. He had a wide range of avoidance tactics at his disposal; sharpening his pencil to a sliver, scribbling on his work, disrupting his neighbours. He was on the special needs register and had a classroom assistant assigned to work with him for a few hours each week. His teacher felt that he was showing little sign of improvement and had requested that the procedure for a Statement of Special Educational Needs be set in motion.

As part of the National Literacy Association's Docklands Learning Acceleration Project, Nicholas, along with the rest of his class, had been assigned an Acorn PocketBook. The school had held a meeting for parents to explain the project. Each parent had signed a contract agreeing to be responsible for the computer on the nights it came home. It was also agreed that when children were bringing the computer home, they would be accompanied to and from school by a parent or carer, as a safety precaution.

Following this meeting the teacher asked the Project team to carry out an introductory activity with a group of children, ready for them to take their computers home that evening. She included Nicholas in the group, but alerted the team to the potential for disruptive behaviour and gave him a warning to be good. After a brief revision of how the computers functioned, Glen Franklin asked the group who they would be most likely to work with at home. Nicholas immediately said: 'Grandad! But he won't know what to do, will he?' 'No, Nicholas,' Glen replied, 'so you'll have to help him.'

Over the next half an hour, Nicholas used his computer to compose a letter to his grandad, explaining how to operate a PocketBook. After break, he returned to the group and, although this was usually the session when he worked with a classroom assistant in another room, he refused to go, saying that he had some more to write. He finished his letter, which is shown as Figure 10.2 with a transcript.

First draft

dear grandad
thisisyou n ers it you pist on or werds
comes up if you what to wert you ners
asdteros if you what to wert to some one
you put the name in. its not a toy notedsg piss
anhget ands to save it.

Transcript

Dear Grandad.

This is how you use it. Press on. All words comes up. If you want to write you use arrows. If you want to write to someone you put the name in. It's not a toy. Don't drop it. Press Acorn and S to save it.

Figure 10.2 Nicholas's Dear Grandad letter

Nicholas's work wasn't perfect. There were spelling mistakes and he had missed out various crucial technical directions. It was obviously a first draft. The important aspect here is that the task was finished because it had a **purpose** and an **audience**, both with a community and not a school focus. Nicholas knew why he was writing and for whom he was writing – a very important person. He had a close relationship with his grandad and this was an opportunity to share an activity with him. More importantly, in this instance Nicholas was the expert; he was going to be the teacher and this gave him a feeling of responsibility and self-esteem.

Was it the use of ICT that brought about this success? Nicholas had taken work home before, but it was usually lost, forgotten or completed inadequately. His parents had told the school that there were frequent arguments about homework and that it caused tension. Why did this succeed when other home/school communications had not?

From the outset there was a firm commitment to see parents as an integral part of the work of the Project, recognising the wealth of evidence that saw the importance of parents/carers as active partners in their children's education. For example, the work of Hancock and Gale in Hackney, described in Wolfendale and Topping (1996), when evaluating the reasons why schools should set up home–school reading programmes, noted the reciprocal benefit to all concerned. Parents became more informed about what happened in school. Teachers had opportunities to learn about literacy practices in the home and community. Children benefited from a shared set of attitudes and expectations which offered security in learning. If this was the case in reading, could not the same apply to the use of computers?

Sanger *et al.* (1997) explored the use and effect of screen–based technologies in home and at school. They noted parental attitudes to computers: 'Well, it's the computer age now isn't it? Got to be able to use them, haven't they?' (mother of 6-year-old).

Immediately the perception of parents and carers is that what their children are doing will be useful to them in their future careers. In the Docklands Project, we found that parents generally agreed with this idea and were pleased to see that their children were being given an opportunity to work with computers. The majority of the children in the project came from homes with no PCs, although many children (particularly boys) were familiar with computer games such as Game Boy and Nintendo.

The Project attempted to make a clear distinction between technology and literacy. We wanted the PocketBook to be **the tool** not **the task**. This distinction often became blurred, and not just in the eyes of teachers. The Project evaluation report (Scott *et al.* 1997) noted that OFSTED reports of schools inspected during the project referred, in most cases, to the project as an ICT initiative.

While not denying that computers do bring with them their technical foibles (and recognising that printers *can* run out of ink at the most inopportune times), the team felt strongly that the project had to be a whole–school literacy initiative and not the sole domain of the ICT coordinator. We particularly targeted English coordinators. With the imminent arrival of the National Literacy Strategy, we looked specifically at matching English tasks to the DfEE National Literacy Strategy Framework for Teaching (1998), and devised computer-based activities to support these. The focus was on the **task** and not the **machine**.

The introduction and use of ICT in the project appeared to be popular with parents; it was recognisable to them as a life-skill that would be invaluable to their children in the future, as school-based 'literacy-skills' in their broadest sense had failed to do. This was evident at the initial parents meetings held in all the Project schools. Parents were invited to attend a meeting in order to accept responsibility for the computer on the evenings their children brought one home. It was made a proviso that children could not take a computer home unless the parents had attended this initial meeting. This proved to be an effective strategy (even though many thought the computers would 'disappear' – in fact very few did) and brought in many families:

'Everybody signed a letter and every child took one home, which was a really good thing because we have a lot of problems here getting parents in because of language and cultural barriers.'

(Scott *et al.* 1997, Project Evaluation Report, Page 50)

However, the Project team became aware that many parents, particularly mothers, were reluctant to become actually involved. The technology could be off-putting; what if it went wrong? 'I'm frightened I might break it,' one mother said.

It seemed as if parents were willing for their children to become computer-literate, but didn't feel that they could become active participants themselves. We were aware that 'the child as expert' was important, but not always enough if the parents were too wary of the technology. Sending the PocketBooks home could be counter-productive, ending with the same kinds of homework arguments that had occurred in Nicholas's home, if we did not raise the skills base of all those (teachers, classroom assistants and parents) working alongside the children. The Project team began running accredited 'parent workshops' in a number of the schools, introducing the basic operating procedures of the computers as well as giving parents some ideas and activities they could try out at home.

These workshops produced very positive results. In one school, where the teacher had been reluctant to send the computers home, parents were going in and asking for them. Another school reported that parents from other classes had been asking when it would be their turn. The quality of interaction between parent and child became more focused and purposeful. In some cases the parents really caught the 'ICT bug':

'When I got home I was sitting with my daughter doing the puzzles...I used to sit for there for ages ... she'd say "It's my turn, mum".' (Scott *et al.* 1997 Project Evaluation Report, Page 51)

Following the introductory workshops, some of the schools invited parents to come in and work with children using their PocketBooks or to support children using the *Integrated Learning Systems* program. Many of the parents involved, expressed how much more confident they felt using technology now. One school suffered mixed feelings when one of their parent volunteers said she couldn't come into school and help any more as she'd enrolled on a computer training course!

The most successful work with parents and carers came about because the **task was clear** and the **purpose was evident**, as advocated by Franklin in a National Literacy Association homework publication (1998). Parents needed to know why the work had been set, how it supported the class work and how this work would be used on return to school. Sending the PocketBooks home without a clear, purposeful task soon devalued the impact of the computers (which were not, after all, equipped with 'super', multimedia games) and relegated them to the status of a toy that had lost its newness. Teachers, along with the Project team, devised activities linked to class plans and teaching objectives for work at home; work for both children and their parents/carers. Some of these were 'one-off' recognisable activities, such as exploring the anagram facility to unscramble a list of words, using a database for recording reading and book reviews and using the same facility to enable children to plan their writing and discover some characteristics of story-structure. Others were more topic based, such as collecting data for some work on electricity in the home. These focused activities, coupled with the keen parental response to computer use, as noted above, helped to make the work successful.

Why did ICT succeed here when other more tried and tested methods had failed in the past? Wolfendale (1983) noted that in education the teacher as professional tended to take a lead when meeting with parents, who then viewed themselves as passive recipients of the school's ideas. The difference with using PocketBooks was that there were no experts! Everybody involved – parents, children and teachers – came new to the technology and, for once, the educational playing field was level. Everyone was learning together. It was a common occurrence in Project schools for the day to begin with 'guess what we found out how to do last night'. The Project team learned many little technical tricks from the children themselves! In the best case scenario, this equality (child and adult), established home–school partnership-practice that was both ongoing, mutually supportive and had real purpose.

Not all the schools in the Project were able to involve parents and carers. There were various reasons for this, for example, a change of teacher midway through the project, teachers' own insecurity with the technology, or unresolved management issues such as battery provision and printer access. The Project team found that in schools where the senior management team took an active interest in the Project these issues were dealt with, for example one school assigned a classroom assistant to the Project class in order to assist with printing and signing the equipment in and out. Another school allocated time first thing in the morning for willing Year 6 pupils to come and assist with downloading work from the

PocketBooks to the PCs. Following the training for parents and carers run by the Project team, Franklin and Carter (1997), who involved parents in the management of sending the PocketBooks home, noted:

> 'All my real success stories are with children who have parental support. It is such a boost to their self-esteem'. (page 19)

There is currently much concern about the underachievement of boys, backed by analysis of statistics from SATs scores for 1998 which show that boys are still falling behind girls in both writing and reading. There is a significant difference in writing at Key Stage 2. QCA (1998) noted that in SATs, 43 per cent of writing is at level 3 or below, but 55 per cent of boys' writing is at level 3 or below. It was noted by Scott *et al.* (1997) that teachers in the Project found that fathers were more willing to become involved with their children's work on PocketBooks than with written homework. Boys generally appeared more motivated to write using the word processor, especially when this could be accompanied by showing off technical know-how such as using the Thesaurus or cut and paste facilities. Boys also preferred to print out their work, downloading to the PC in order to format the text. Interestingly, girls, while willing to use their computers to gather their information, were heard to express preference to hand writing for final drafts, saying that it looked 'nicer'. Several parents also expressed concern about handwriting.

Following the work of Wray and Lewis (1997), the Project team developed activities using writing frames. The purchase of SDD discs for the PocketBooks at the latter stages of the project enabled teachers to share a collection of multipurpose frames, which could be used to structure children's writing. The frames provided templates of starters, connectives and sentence modifiers which scaffolded the children's writing in a particular text-type (Derewianka 1990). The project focused initially on fiction text level work exploring character, plot structure and key events in stories, before developing into non-fiction, for example comparing fact and opinion in comparative newspaper reports.

Providing writing frames proved particularly useful as a homework strategy. Parents had a clear idea of what was expected, rather than being presented with a blank screen and an unclear purpose. Teachers found that children who were struggling or unwilling writers, or who used English as an additional language achieved greater success when supported by writing frames; a finding also noted by Wray and Lewis. The example shown in Figure 10.3 shows one child's writing, developing from first to final draft using a writing frame provided on his computer.

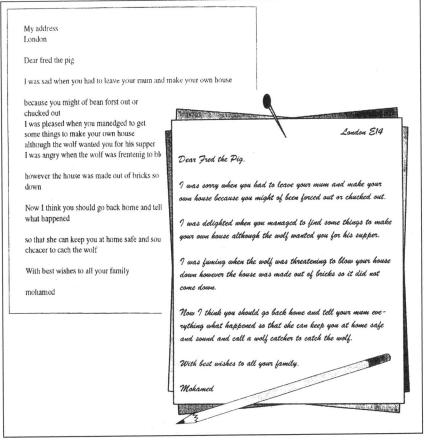

Figures 10.3 Two versions of Fred the Pig

Conclusion

One comment from a delegate at a seminar given by a member of the Project team was, 'Well, all this can be done on paper'. In the majority of cases he was right! Why then did we use computers and why do we continue, after the conclusion of the Docklands Project, to advocate their use as a tool for Literacy? The NLA Project team advocated the 4 E's of ICT. Does the technology:

1. Ease and support the task in hand?

It is easy to become technologically led. There are many exciting new CD-ROMs which dazzle by the quality, presentation and extensive content. As more parents become computer-confident, they too will be buying such items, with a view to supporting their children's learning at home. We need to look beyond the dazzle and consider carefully how the computer supports the task or learning objective. It is, we must keep reminding ourselves, a tool, and needs to be used for a purpose. Finding one's way around some of the software, fun though it may be, does not help when needing to track down answers to specific questions. Children need both the technical skills and the information retrieval skills to use ICT effectively.

2. Enable the learner?

Computers make no judgements about the ability or the approaches of the user. They have no expectations. The learner is therefore in control of the learning environment. With this comes the security to experiment, to try out new ideas, spellings and vocabulary, using the electronic gadgetry. The PocketBook is small; only the user can see the screen. This privacy allows the learner to take risks, and to seek help when ready. No rubbing out or untidy writing. Changes can be made easily. Scaffolded writing using frames and templates supports the less confident writer or user of English. Franklin and Carter (1997) noted that parents and carers saw a different, more positive approach to spelling and drafting. Suddenly there was no such thing as failure.

3. Ensure that learning outcomes can be achieved?

Work from children like Nicholas indicates how computer technology can enthuse and motivate even the most reluctant writer, but it is important that we look beyond this and consider what learning has actually taken place. Sharing the work at home, allows the child to share and build on the work in school. As the studies of Donald Graves (1989) have shown, explaining the task to another enables the child to consolidate the learning and build on existing knowledge.

4. Enhance the quality and value of the task?

Earlier, we discussed children's attitude to the presentation of their work. We as educationalists are often guilty of judging the quality of a piece by its look, not its content. The power of the printed word is that judgements cannot be made by a cursory glance; it could have been written by anyone of any age or ability. The focus is on the content. All the hard work is not dismissed with a 'could be neater'. The spin-off from this is that we must now encourage children to look beyond the neat presentation and to become critical readers of their own writing. The elements of drafting and proof-reading featured in the text level strand of the National Literacy Strategy (1998) are enhanced by the use of word processing. Redrafting is not seen as a meaningless ritual, but rather as an improvement of the original, as children become more aware of the qualities of their writing and parents play a more proactive role in the redrafting process.

We recognise that schools are not stable environments. Teachers come and go, new initiatives arrive with increasing regularity, ICT is continually changing, upgrading and developing. Schools are being linked to the Internet and a nation-wide programme of training is about to be implemented. It would not be surprising if the involvement of parents and carers was pushed lower down the scale of priorities in schools. Adding portable computers to this already overburdened scenario, may be seen as the proverbial last straw.

The work of the Docklands Project and the NLA found that ICT provided a change of approach to tried and tested ideas; offered structure and support for less able children and extended those at the top end; gave a new insight to vocabulary and word work; gave children a more positive approach to drafting and editing; and motivated and encouraged a fresh response to the skills of reading and writing. It involved parents as equal partners for once, in a new learning process, which was mutually beneficial to all concerned. Children often became those with most power in the learning relationship. It enabled dialogue to be established, gave a real and lasting purpose and focus to homework, and home–school partnerships. All of these factors led to an undeniable improvement in literacy standards for Docklands residents and schools were changed. An American proverb says, 'You always get what you've always had, if you always do what you've always done!' The catalyst of ICT, empowering all groups in the Docklands partnership, had been the innovative process as well as the innovative solution.

References

Chavkin, N. F. and Williams, D. L. Jr. (1985) *Parent Involvement in Education Project: Executive summary of the final report*. Austin, Texas: Southwest Educational Development Laboratory.

Dauber, S. L. and Epstein, J. L. (1989) 'Parent attitudes and practices of involvement in inner-city elementary and middle schools'. Paper presented at the annual meeting of the American Educational Research Association, San Francisco.

Davies, D. (1989) 'Poor parents, teachers, and the schools: comments about practice, policy and research'. Paper presented at the annual meeting of the American Educational Research Association, San Francisco.

Derewianka, B. (1990) *Exploring How Texts Work*. Sydney: Primary English Teaching Association of New South Wales.

DfEE (1998) *National Literacy Strategy: Framework for Teaching*. London: DfEE.

Epstein, J. L. (1987) 'Toward a theory of family–school connections: teacher practices and parent involvement', in Hurrelmann, K., Kaufmann, F., and Losel, F. (eds), *Social Intervention: Potential and constraints*. New York: deGruyter.

Ernst and Young (1993) *Literacy, Education and Training: Their impact on the UK economy*, mimeo. London: Ernst and Young.

Franklin, G. (1998) 'Homework without headaches', *Perfect Partners.* Christchurch: Questions Publishing and the National Literacy Association.

Franklin, G. and Carter, F. (1997) 'And then, and then, and then', *Literacy for All.* Christchurch: Questions Publishing and the National Literacy Association.

Graves, D. (1989) *Investigating Non-Fiction.* Portsmouth, NH: Heinemann.

Leitch, L. M. and Tangri, S. S. (1988) 'Barriers to home–school collaboration', *Educational Horizons*, **66**, 70–4.

Milne, A. M. (1989) 'Family structure and the achievement of children', in Weston, W. J. (ed.) *Education and the American Family.* New York: New York University Press.

Mortimore, P. *et al.* (1988) *School Matters: The junior years.* Wells: Open Books.

National Literacy Association (1998) *The Pledge for Literacy.* Christchurch: National Literacy Association.

Pappert, S. (1993) *The Children's Machine: Rethinking school in the age of the computer.* San Francisco: Basic Books.

Pappert, S. (1996) *The Connected Family: Bridging the digital generation gap.* San Francisco: Longstreet Press.

Qualifications and Curriculum Authority (1998) *Standards at Key Stage 2 – English, Mathematics and Science.* London: QCA.

Rankin, P. T. (1967) 'The relationship between parent behavior and achievements of inner-city elementary school-children'. Paper presented at the annual meeting of the American Educational Research Association, Washington DC.

Sanger *et al.* (1997) *Young Children, Videos and Computer Games. Issues for teachers and parents.* London: Falmer Press.

Scheerens, J. (1992) *Effective Schooling: Research, theory and practice.* London: Cassell.

Scott, D. *et al.* (1997) *Report of the Evaluation of the NLA Docklands Learning Acceleration Project.* London: London University Institute of Education.

Smith, M. B. (1968) 'School and home: focus on achievement', in Passow, A. H. (ed.) *Developing Programs for the Educationally Disadvantaged.* New York: Teachers College Press.

Snider, W. (1990) 'Parents as partners: adding their voices to decisions on how schools are run', *Education Week* **9**(44), 11–15.

Vollands, S. R., Topping, K. J. and Evans, H. M. (1999) 'Compterized self-assessment of reading comprehension: impact of Accelerated Reader on reading achievement and attitude', *Reading and Writing Quarterly*, **15**(2).

Walberg, H. J., Bole, R. J. and Waxman, H. C. (1980) 'School-based family socialisation and reading achievement in the inner city', *Psychology in the Schools* **17**, 509–14.

Wolfendale, S. (1983) *Parental Participation in Children's Development and Education.* London: Gordon and Breach.

Wolfendale, S. and Topping, K. (eds) (1996) *Family Involvement in Literacy.* London: Cassell Education.

Wray, D. and Lewis, M. (1997) *Extending Literacy.* London: Routledge.

Ysseldyke, J. E. and Christenson, S. L. (1993) *The Instructional Environment System – II. A system to identify a student's instructional needs.* Longman, Col.: Sopris West.

Index